The War Against Children:
South Africa's Youngest Victims

with a Foreword by Bishop Desmond Tutu

Lawyers Committee for Human Rights

36 West 44th Street
New York, New York
10036

ISBN 0-934143-00-5

The Lawyers Committee for Human Rights

Since 1978 the Lawyers Committee has served as a public interest law center. The Lawyers Committee works to promote international human rights and refugee law and legal procedures in the United States and abroad. The chairman of the Lawyers Committee is Marvin E. Frankel; Michael Posner is its Executive Director and Diane Orentlicher is its Deputy Director.

Bound copies of this report are available from:

The Lawyers Committee for Human Rights
36 West 44th Street
New York, NY 10036

The Lawyers Committee gratefully acknowledges the support of the Reed Foundation and the ARCA Foundation in the preparation of this report.

Design by Philmark Lithographics

TABLE OF CONTENTS

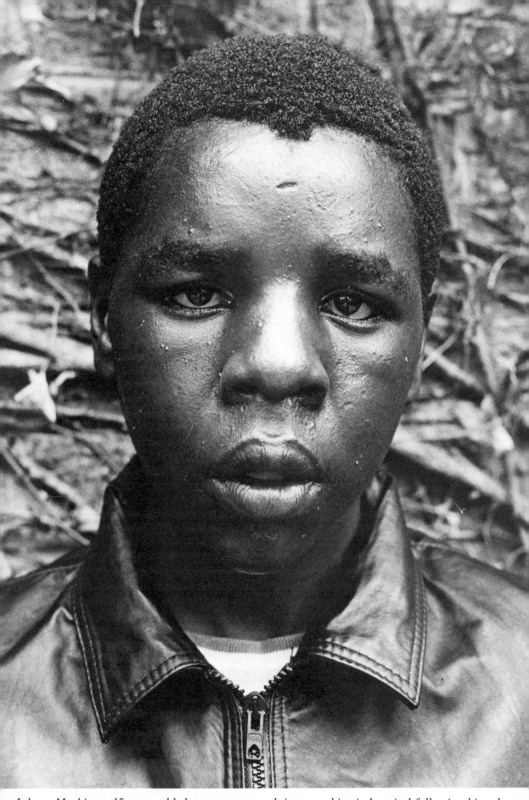

Johnny Mashiane, 15 years old, has spent a month in a psychiatric hospital following his release from detention. A normal child before his arrest, he is now barely able to speak. (Gill de Vlieg, courtesy of Afrapix.)

FOREWORD

By

The Right Reverend Desmond Mpilo Tutu

I have seen the Johnny referred to in this book. He spoke with great difficulty as if his tongue was swollen and filled his mouth. He had a kind of lisp as well. His eyes were dull as of someone who seemed to be dead to the world for much of the time. When he walked it was with a slow painful shuffle like a punchdrunk ex-boxer. And when I saw him I wanted to cry but most of all I was filled with a blazing anger against a system that could do this to a child in the bloom of youth who had all his life in front of him. It made me resolve that I had to do all that God would enable me to do to help destroy the evil system which could perpetrate such atrocities just in order to defend itself.

Johnny is real. He used to be a lively youngster, full of life and fun until he fell into the clutches of the security system of the apartheid regime. It is not quite clear what the police did to Johnny. Perhaps it does not matter any longer. What is certain is that he went in a lively, healthy and normal youngster and he came out a walking human vegetable. The police did something to him.

It is quite important for the world to know that Johnny is no figment of a feverish imagination. I saw him with my own eyes in Khotso House, Johannesburg. It is important for the world to know this because the stock response, almost like a Pavlovian conditioned reflex, of the South African Government, especially of the Minister of Law and Order, when confronted with such evidence is to say it is totally unsubstantiated and it is mere allegation designed to discredit the police in a deliberate smear-campaign. The world should bear in mind that this gentleman was the same one who, when faced with the evidence that his police had shot an unarmed peaceful funeral procession at Langa near Uitenhage on the anniversary of Sharpeville, March 21st 1985, quickly sprang to the defence of his men by asserting that the black crowd was angry and aggressive and that many were carrying stones and petrol bombs. This ministerial assertion was shown to be totally at variance with the truth when the Kannemeyer Commission reported. What the Minister of Law and Order says has to be treated with considerable caution.

Even if all the other cases referred to in this study were untrue, Johnny's case alone ought to be enough to fill any decent person who cares about human rights, and especially the rights of defenceless children, with revulsion and indignation. It should galvanise such a person into the kind of action that will ensure that such dastardly deeds will not easily be repeated with so much impunity and disregard for the feelings of others.

The other cases have either been personally investigated by the author through her interviews and unless we were to impugn her integrity by charging her with fabricating the evidence we are compelled to accept their veracity; or they have been culled from newspaper reports. The author has indicated the veritable minefield which journalists have to negotiate in South Africa when they report on any matter relating to the police, prisons and the Defence Force. Consequently when anything has appeared in the press and not been challenged by the authorities you can be sure that what has been reported is substantially true.

But nobody who has a television set needs to be convinced about the brutality of the South African Police and security forces which was depicted daily worldwide until the Government slapped a ban on that kind of reporting of the unrest in South Africa. No one with a T.V. screen can say the "Trojan horse" incident was unsubstantiated allegation. The world saw policemen hiding in crates on a delivery lorry to serve as a decoy to lure children in a tense riot area to stone and, when some did, the police came out with guns blazing cowboy-style and children were killed.

This study is not intended to discredit the South African Police and other security forces. It is a clinical account, well-documented and researched, of what has been happening to children who have been victims of the violence that has been unleashed in our beautiful but oh so sad land by the vicious policy of apartheid.

I hope you will have the stomach to read it, and will not allow your anger to be dissipated in some gesture of helplessness. I hope you will be galvanized into action that will topple apartheid and help establish a dispensation which is just, stable, democratic and safe for all our children, black and white.

Johannesburg, South Africa
April 1986

PREFACE

This report examines recent abuses of human rights in South Africa against children under the age of 18 years.[1] The report is based on two fact-finding missions to South Africa undertaken by Helena Cook of the Lawyers Committee for Human Rights. Ms. Cook's first visit took place from June 19 to July 24, 1985. Her second visit took place from November 3 through 28, 1985.

While in South Africa, Ms. Cook met with a substantial number of ex-detainees and victims of human rights violations in Johannesburg, Durban, Port Elizabeth and Cape Town. She also had extensive discussions with judges, lawyers, church representatives, human rights workers, doctors, members of youth and community organizations in the townships, teachers, Members of Parliament, journalists and businessmen. Ms. Cook met with representatives of the United States government in Durban, Cape Town and Pretoria and with State Department officials in Washington.

In gathering information for this report, Ms. Cook worked closely with two leading human rights organizations in South Africa -- the Black Sash and the Detainees' Parents Support Committee. Both groups have been active in compiling extensive information about human rights abuses in South Africa, and in providing advice and practical assistance to the victims of these abuses.

The conclusions of this report are based largely on interviews, signed statements or sworn affidavits given by victims, their families and eyewitnesses of the human rights violations described herein. Wherever possible, allegations of such violations were checked against official documents, corroborating testimony and other source materials. While every allegation could not be substantiated with certainty,

---

1. For the purpose of this report we have followed the definition in the South African Child Care Act (Act No. 74 of 1983), the basic statute that deals with the welfare and protection of children by the state. According to Section 1(v) of that Act, "child means any person under the age of 18 years."

several clear patterns emerged in the course of our investigations. They are the subject of this report.

The overwhelming majority of the victims and witnesses who were interviewed or whose testimonies were made available to us have requested anonymity, fearing reprisals and harassment. We have respected those requests and have not used their real names. These requests are indicative of the level of official repression and violence within South Africa's security apparatus.

We wish to thank all those in South Africa who have assisted in the preparation of this report, often at personal risk to themselves, and whose names cannot be mentioned here in the interest of their own safety. We are particularly grateful to the Black Sash, Detainees' Parents Support Committee, Legal Resources Center, Black Lawyers Association and Center for Applied Legal Studies for their cooperation in the compilation of this report. The Lawyers Committee also gratefully acknowledges the assistance of Ms. Dayle Powell of the Carter Center of Emory University in Atlanta, who generously shared her experiences and the results of her interviews with children in South Africa.

The principal author of this report was Helena Cook. Diane Orentlicher, Deputy Director of the Lawyers Committee, also made a substantial contribution to it. Special thanks are owed to Milagro Harris, Patricia McCrary and Bayla Travis for their assistance in the preparation of this report.

New York
April 1986

INTRODUCTION

For the past 19 months South Africa has been wracked by the worst outbreak of violence in the history of the republic. More than 1400 people have been killed; almost all were black. The violence comes at a time of increased political opposition to the government within the black community, and escalating discontent and civil unrest within the black townships.[1] The South African government's response to the unrest has been a ruthless campaign to crush all opposition, to suppress dissenting voices and to hinder the news media's efforts to report what is happening. In July 1985 a State of Emergency was declared in areas most affected by the unrest. It remained in effect for eight months.

As happened in Soweto a decade ago, children and young people in the townships have been in the forefront of protests against apartheid and the resultant repression of the country's black majority. They have become apartheid's youngest victims. Far from being spared the brunt of repression, children have often been singled out as special targets of state-sanctioned violence. Consider these recent incidents:

- Joseph is a shy, quiet boy, only 14 years old. The fingernails of one of his hands are twisted and blackened, the result of electric shock treatment to which soldiers subjected him many times during the days he was kept, along with other children, at an army camp outside Daveyton. His wrist is scarred where he was burned with a cigarette lighter. His leg bears a wound where it was cut by soldiers with a broken soft drink bottle. Joseph was blindfolded when he was first picked up by the soldiers on September 19, 1985 while playing football and does not know exactly where the camp

----

1. These are the segregated residential areas set aside under the policy of apartheid for black South Africans. They are generally isolated from the privileged white areas and many have only minimal facilities in the way of water, electricity, sanitation and other amenities.

is. For nine days, the soldiers terrorized Joseph and the other children they had picked up with him.

- Four year-old Mitah Ngobeni was shot on September 10, 1985 by a rubber bullet while playing in the yard of her home in Atteridgeville. Although rubber bullets are supposed to be non-lethal, Mitah died of skull and brain damage and excessive blood loss.

- Thirteen year-old Moses Mope was on his way to church on October 21, 1985 with friends when a car pulled up beside the group. The children started to flee, but Moses was grabbed by a white policeman, who savagely beat and trampled on the young boy. A neighbor took Moses home, covered with blood. "When I touched his stomach, he pulled away in agony," his father told a reporter. "I also noticed his jaw was cracked and he was injured on the head and other parts of the body." Moses was only semi-conscious and died on the way to the hospital.

Joseph, Mitah and Moses are entries on a long and growing list of children under the age of 18 years who have been killed or injured by South African security forces in recent months. They are victims of a deliberate government strategy to suppress the nation's growing unrest primarily through the use of force.

A substantial portion of the violence against children has been a response to the protests voiced by student organizations. Mobilized initially in opposition to an inadequate and discriminatory educational system, which budgets seven times as much for each white child as for an African child,[2] students have taken up the fundamental

----

2. Under the system of apartheid, South Africans are classified at birth as belonging to one of four different racial groups -- White, Colored (mixed-race), Asian and Black (African). This classification determines and controls every aspect of people's lives, including where they can live, go to school, work and whether they can vote. The African majority constitutes 73.8% of the population, Whites make up 14.8% and Coloreds and Asians

political demands of the black[3] majority that underlie the unrest. The primary means of organized protest used by children during the unrest has been the school boycott. Occurring sporadically in 1983, school boycotts became increasingly widespread and sustained in 1984 and 1985, reaching a peak during the State of Emergency.

Military troops, first brought in to assist the police in the townships in October 1984, now routinely assist in all manner of policing operations. The security forces have transformed the townships into virtual war zones. Their conduct is provocative and confrontational in an intensive campaign to break the boycotts, crush student organizations and force children back to school. The pervasive and indiscriminate nature of these policing operations has made it virtually inevitable that innocent children would fall within their sweep.

The violence was aggravated by stringent emergency regulations imposed during the eight-month State of Emergency. Under those measures the government imposed a sweeping press ban and gave the security forces vitually a free hand in controlling the townships, shielded by a blanket indemnity against legal proceedings arising out of their conduct during the unrest.

More than 200 children have been killed in the past year and hundreds more have been injured by the security forces' excessive and reckless use of tear gas, birdshot, rubber bullets, sjamboks[4] and even live ammunition to combat the unrest.

In large-scale and often arbitrary police action, thousands of children, some as young as seven years old, have been arrested and detained pursuant to South Africa's sweeping security and criminal legislation. On occasion,

----

constitute 8.7% and 2.7% respectively. Race Relations Survey 1984, South African Institute of Race Relations, 1985.

3. Throughout this report the word "black" is used to denote all three non-white population groups, Colored, Asian and Black. South Africans classified by the apartheid regime as "Black" are referred to herein as "African."

4. A sjambok is heavy hide whip with a metal tip routinely used by the police.

entire schools have been arrested en masse. During the State of Emergency, more than 2000 children under the age of 16 were detained under the emergency regulations. Others have been held in solitary confinement pursuant to the Internal Security Act, a permanent law, allegedly as threats to state security. Serious criminal charges have been laid against numerous children, frequently on highly insufficient evidence, in connection with incidents of rioting or unrest. Many of these children, who face severe custodial sentences if convicted, appear in court without any legal representation.

Children arrested by the security forces are routinely assaulted with fists, rifle butts and sjamboks. Some have been badly tortured while in custody. Sixteen year-old Eugene underwent surgery after only five days in security detention, during which he was repeatedly beaten and subjected to electric shocks while undergoing intensive interrogation. Johnny, age 15, spent a month in a psychiatric hospital after his release from custody. Although friends say he was perfectly normal before his arrest, he is now mentally scarred and barely able to communicate.

Although the State of Emergency was lifted on March 7, 1986, the violence continues. Military troops continue to be deployed in many townships and the State President has warned that even greater forces will be used in the townships if necessary. More than 100 people have been killed since the lifting of the Emergency, and the daily average death toll of five is now the highest it has been at any time during the unrest. The government has recently indicated that some of the extraordinary powers accorded security forces during the State of Emergency will be incorporated into the ordinary law of the land.

Nor has the government made any significant progress in addressing the long-standing grievances of the black majority that are fueling the unrest. While school boycotts have been temporarily suspended, the students have indicated that this is conditional on their grievances being addressed. An imminent resumption of the school boycotts is now a strong possibility, which signals a probable increase in the repression of children.

Increasingly, the people of South Africa, including her youth, have come to view the United States government as part of the problem. They perceive the Administration's policy of "constructive engagement," which relies principally on quiet diplomacy rather than forceful criticism, as active support for the regime that denies their basic rights. Nobel Peace laureate Bishop Desmond Tutu spoke for most black South Africans when he said,"We will not forget where the American Administration stood at a time when we needed them desperately."

Public and congressional pressure in the last year has forced the Administration to take a more critical public posture toward the policies of apartheid. In March 1986, for the first time, Chester Crocker, the Assistant Secretary of State for African Affairs, publicly stated that the Administration supports majority rule in South Africa. Unfortunately, this pronouncement was immediately rebuked by the White House, which said that it did not reflect official policy. The United States government has also failed to condemn South Africa's war against children in a manner commensurate with the severity of the current situation.

A generation of children is growing up in South Africa knowing nothing but the daily violence of the white minority regime. They have witnessed the deaths of relatives and schoolfriends. Many have themselves come under brutal attack or have been arrested and detained. Their education has been seriously disrupted and their lives turned upside down. These children feel nothing but hatred, bitterness and fear toward the security forces. Unless concerted international pressure is brought to bear on the government of South Africa, from the United States and elsewhere, the future of these children, and with it the future of South Africa, looks bleak.

Summary of Conclusions

1. Throughout the ongoing civil unrest in South Africa, children often have been the special target of security force violence. In their frequent patrols through black townships, security forces have singled out children for arrest, pursuing them with whips, and shooting any child who runs away. In other cases, children have been caught in the perpetual crossfire of confrontations in areas where they live, play and go to school.

2. Many children have lost their lives in confrontations with the police and the army, some killed by the supposedly non-lethal weapons -- tear gas, rubber bullets and buckshot -- that are used indiscriminately and recklessly in police operations in the townships.

3. Many more children have been injured, some permanently damaged, by security forces. Children who are shot risk arrest if they seek medical treatment; security forces maintain an armed guard at some hospitals where they arrest anyone with birdshot or buckshot wounds. As a result, parents are often afraid to seek even urgent medical treatment for their wounded children.

4. The South African Defense Force, now permanently deployed in the troubled townships, is responsible for many of the abuses. Soldiers frequently pick up children on the streets, load them into armored vehicles, and subject the children to threats, intimidation and torture before releasing them or handing them over to the police. Soldiers also have abducted children, held them in nearby army barracks for several days, and savagely tortured them. Such abuse has included burning children's flesh, subjecting them to electric shock, submerging them in sewage water, and whipping them.

5. Black schools are the site of frequent and often violent confrontations between the security forces and school children. Pupils have been killed and injured in these brutal attacks by police and army units. Schools have also been the site of mass arrests of children, some as young as seven years old.

6. Children, including the very young, have been arrested and detained in large numbers under permanent security legislation, the emergency regulations in effect during the State of Emergency and the criminal legislation. Many of these arrests are arbitrary and indiscriminate. Parents generally are not informed of their child's arrest and are not permitted access to the child in custody.

7. Children arrested on serious criminal charges that carry a potentially heavy custodial sentence are appearing in the courts without legal representation. Charges often are based on weak or wholly fabricated evidence. Bail for these children is set at impossibly high amounts or is refused outright.

8. Severe torture is routinely inflicted upon children who are arrested and detained. Assault at the time of arrest and in the early days of detention is common, sometimes resulting in serious injuries. Attacks at the time of arrest typically include punching, whipping, kicking and beating with rifle butts. Similar abuses, as well as tear gassing, is inflicted during detention as a punishment or a technique of interrogation. Torture also takes place on a massive scale while prisoners are detained, and children have not been spared. Some young victims have been physically and mentally scarred by their experiences in custody.

9. At least three children, including a 13 year-old, died in detention during 1985 as a result of police abuse.

10. Children in custody are sometimes kept in cells with adult criminals, who at times have subjected the children to beatings and sexual abuse. Food,

and sometimes water, has been denied children in prison, and they frequently are barred from access to parents and lawyers.

11. Investigation and prosecution of the security forces for these abuses is virtually unknown. The South African government has been unresponsive to complaints about police and army conduct, and has made no discernible effort to restrain or discipline the security forces.

Chapter I

Background to the Unrest

The conflict that has torn the country for more than 18 months has, for the most part, been centered in the major urban townships, but has spread to some of the more rural areas as well. It has involved all sectors of these communities, including labour, church and student groups, as well as a broad range of community and civic organizations. Thousands of township residents, including children, have participated in boycotts, strikes, marches and other forms of protest to demonstrate their opposition to apartheid and to the brutal methods used to enforce it.

The latest period of unrest, rooted in the continuing injustices and humiliations of the basic system of apartheid, was triggered by the implementation of a new Constitution in South Africa in 1984. That Constitution extended political representation in central government, hitherto restricted to whites, to the Colored and Asian population groups, but continued to exclude the African majority from participation. It also considerably strengthened the executive arm of government under a powerful State President and entrenched the domination of the white minority in government.

Rising black anger against the Constitution and the government's much-vaunted "reformist" stance, perceived by many to be no more than an attempt to perpetuate the fundamental policies of apartheid while presenting it in a more acceptable form for the international community, erupted in a mass protest campaign. This effort was spearheaded by a new non-parliamentary opposition group, the United Democratic Front (UDF). This multi-racial umbrella organization comprises some 600 affiliated groups committed to a "united and democratic" South Africa.

A highly successful boycott of the elections to the new Parliament in August 1984 was followed by an outbreak of protests and demonstrations. Residents of the nation's townships, the segregated residential areas set aside for black South Africans, took to the streets to voice their grievances against the government. These included the inadequate and inferior education system for black children, steep increases in rent for state-owned housing units, rising utility charges and taxes, as well as increases in the cost of transport and essential commodities at a time of wide-spread unemployment and deepening economic recession.

Much of the anger has been directed at the discredited and unrepresentative local town councils. Instituted in 1983, the councils were part of a government reform initiative aimed at providing more autonomous local government for Africans. They have been widely rejected by township residents, primarily because this "reform" was seen as an attempt to deflect the fundamental demand of the African majority for political participation in central government.[5]

Protests during the unrest have assumed various forms, including consumer boycotts, marches and demonstrations, strikes and work "stay-aways," as well as sporadic outbreaks of rioting, property damage and violent attacks against those perceived to be government collaborators. The primary method of protest employed by school children and students has been the boycott of classes at schools and universities.

The school boycotts, which started in 1983, were initially undertaken in support of calls for reform of the black educational system, which lags far behind the white school system. The students' demands were virtually the same as those that sparked the Soweto uprisings ten years earlier, and which recur time and again but are never adequately addressed by the government. These include free, compulsory education for all children, better qualified teachers, free and appropriate text books and educational materials, the recognition of democratically-elected student

----

5. The councillors were also rejected because they were responsible for many of the increased rents and charges being demanded of the residents. The government failed to provide the new councils with adequate resources for the provision of public services. Because of this, the councils were forced to raise rents and charges beyond the means of many township residents.

representative councils and an end to excessive corporal punishment and the sexual harassment of girl pupils.

In 1984, students increasingly linked their demands to the broader political grievances underlying the wave of discontent that swept through many of the black communities that year. Many had concluded that meaningful improvements in black education must be preceded by major changes in the apartheid system as a whole. Thus, on the day of the Colored parliamentary elections under the new Constitution, 800,000 pupils and students boycotted classes nation-wide. The school boycotts spread rapidly throughout the country in 1984 and 1985, and reached a peak in the period following the declaration of the State of Emergency on July 21, 1985 and leading up to the end-of-year examinations in November 1985.

While many have resorted to non-violent forms of protest, others have used violence to press their demands. Demonstrations have turned to rioting. Blacks seen as "collaborators" with the hated white regime, including some town councillors and policemen, have been attacked; some have been killed. Children have thrown stones at the heavily armored casspirs that patrol their streets, and property belonging to the state or perceived "collaborators" has been destroyed.

The South African government's response to political organization and to all forms of protest has been repressive, excessive, and indiscriminately violent. Military troops were brought into the townships late in 1984 and have become a permanent feature of policing operations there. Peaceful dissent has been silenced with brute force. Children who throw stones at armored vehicles or run away from the security forces are shot on sight. The government shows no indication to discipline its forces or respond to calls for official investigations into their conduct.

As the conflict intensified during 1985, even in the face of increasingly violent methods employed by the security forces to contain it, the State President, Mr. P.W. Botha, declared a State of Emergency in 36 magisterial districts on July 21, 1985. The affected districts were black townships located mainly in the Transvaal and the Eastern Cape. As the unrest spread rapidly to the Western Cape, the

State of Emergency was extended on October 26, 1985 to cover many of the townships in that area of the country as well.

The State of Emergency lasted for nearly eight months, and was finally lifted on March 7, 1986. During this period, special emergency regulations gave the security forces virtually unchecked power to control the townships, and the repression intensified alarmingly. The average daily death toll rose to 3.44, from a pre-Emergency average in 1985 of 1.67. A total of 7996 people were arrested and detained under the enlarged powers of detention without charge given to the security forces. A blanket indemnity granted to the security forces, and severe restrictions imposed on media coverage of the unrest, removed practically the only remaining restraints on the police and the army.

Much of the state-instituted violence and repression against children has been part of a strategy to break the boycotts and crush student organization and protest. In August 1985, orders under the emergency regulations were issued that required pupils to be in the classrooms during school hours;[6] prohibited any activities that did not have a direct bearing on tuition; prevented anyone other than pupils or staff from entering school premises; and forbade the teaching or communication of any matter falling outside the official syllabus or normal school activities.

On August 28, 1985, one of the most popular and broad-based organizations of both primary and high school students, the Congress of South African Students (COSAS), was banned. COSAS had long been the focus of the authorities' attempts to crush student resistance. Since its inception in 1979, many of its members have been either killed in clashes with the police, detained or forced into hiding. Some have mysteriously disappeared. After the banning of COSAS, Divisional Police Commissioner in Soweto, Brigadier Jan Coetzee, warned: "Trouble will escalate in the schools unless member of COSAS are all

----

6. It is ironic that special orders had to be issued to require black children to attend school. Compulsory education has been one of the key demands of black students for more than 20 years.

rounded up by the security forces . . . . [T]he police will never rest until they are all arrested."[7] By mid-September 1985, the Detainees' Parents Support Committee noted that one out of every five detainees was a member of COSAS.

The security forces have resorted to harsh measures to break the boycotts and force children back to school. Police and army units have stormed onto school premises armed with tear gas, rubber bullets, birdshot, sjamboks and live ammunition, arresting anyone suspected of participating in or organizing the boycotts. Peaceful marches and meetings organized by the pupils have been violently broken up by police. Numerous children have been injured, and some have been killed in these confrontations. Children of all ages in the townships, regardless of their involvement in the protests, are constantly at risk of arrest, assault and even death.

The serious abuses perpetrated against children show no sign of diminishing. In December last year a national educational conference was convened by the National Education Crisis Committee, a group formed at the end of 1985 in response to the serious educational crisis resulting from the continuing boycotts. Resolutions adopted at the conference, which was attended by 160 community and student organizations, encouraged pupils to return to school at the end of January 1986. Although the majority of pupils agreed to this, the return to school has not restored peace. On January 27, 1986, in police confrontations in Kagiso on the West Rand, a 15 year-old school girl, Franscina Legoete, was killed and 13 other pupils were hospitalized with injuries. In the last week of February, 40 pupils were arrested and detained in Bonteheuvel in the Cape Province, and students were detained in six other townships. Clashes with police in some schools in the Eastern Transvaal have already led to a resumption of the boycott there.

The return to school in January was expressly conditional upon certain key demands of the students being met by the government by the end of March 1986. These included the lifting of the State of Emergency, the withdrawal of army troops from the townships, the

----

7. Weekly Mail, September 6, 1985.

unbanning of COSAS, the release of detained teachers and students, the rescheduling of examination dates and the establishment of democratic student representative councils in schools.

Apart from the lifting of the State of Emergency on March 7, 1986, there have been no substantial steps taken toward meeting these demands. A subsequent conference of the National Education Crisis Committee held on March 30, 1986 urged pupils to remain in school, but this appeal was coupled with calls for township residents to use consumer and rent boycotts to back student demands. In addition, a national "stay-away," or general strike, has been called for mid-June 1986, which will mark the 10th anniversary of the Soweto uprisings.

The continued intransigence of the South African government toward the students is likely to lead to a resumption of school boycotts in the coming months, particularly if the violence against children continues unabated. A student representative in the Western Cape explained:

> Our schools can never be normal again. Too many of our people have been killed, injured or detained in our struggle for a decent education. Our memories are filled with the sacrifices our parents and students have made.

CHAPTER II

The Apparatus of Control

South Africa's system of apartheid is maintained by a sophisticated, centralized and tightly-woven security apparatus. Its principal *modus operandi* is repression, and a complex web of legislation institutionalizes this approach.

The state's security legislation, together with other statutes, contains measures that provide a high degree of control over organizations, individuals and activities that demonstrate opposition to or criticism of the State. At the same time, these laws minimize public scrutiny of the methods of the security forces.

The extraordinary powers brought into effect by executive proclamation under the State of Emergency last year did not greatly enlarge such measures of control. Instead, they consolidated the implementation of these measures in the hands of the security forces without requiring recourse to a higher authority, and thus widened the already vast potential for abuse.

A. The Security Structure

The security structure in South Africa includes both military and police forces, and operates under the ultimate authority of the State Security Council (SSC). The Council is a Cabinet committee chaired by the State President that comprises senior Cabinet ministers, as well as the defense and security chiefs. Originally established as a consultative committee in 1972, the SSC now plays a central role in formulating and implementing policy and strategy in relation to national security. The SSC meets before the full Cabinet convenes, and some commentators believe it has reduced the decision-making power of the Cabinet. Its decisions, which are submitted to Parliament, already bear the stamp of presidential authority. The Council liaises directly with government departments, and its jurisdiction encompasses virtually every area of government activity.

Potential threats to state security are identified and investigated by the National Intelligence Service (NIS), which reports to the SSC. The NIS is also intended to coordinate the activities of Military Intelligence and the Security Branch of the South African Police. At the same time, the work of the NIS is designed to complement the activities of these two units. While NIS focuses on "overseas operations," internal security matters are the responsibility of the Security Branch, a plainclothes police unit that handles the arrest, detention, interrogation and prosecution of political offenders. As a police unit, the Security Branch is answerable to the Minister of Law and Order, who also sits on the SSC.

The Security Branch has been responsible for serious and pervasive abuses of detainees, sometimes resulting in death. Physical abuse, including torture of detainees by the Security Branch, has typically occurred during interrogation (see Chapter VII, *infra*). The majority of deaths in detention in the past 20 years have occurred while the victims were in the custody of the Security Branch, or very shortly thereafter, in circumstances that strongly point to serious police abuse. There were 12 deaths in detention during 1985, the highest number recorded since detention without trial was incorporated into the security legislation more than 20 years ago.

B. The South African Police

The South African Police (SAP) is a regular force responsible for enforcing law and order and for riot control. As such, the SAP has been centrally involved in controlling the townships throughout the unrest. The SAP comprises some 45,000 men and women, of whom approximately 50% are white, 39% are African and the remainder are Indian and Colored. In October 1984 the Minister of Law and Order announced plans to increase the police force by more than 50% over the next ten years.

The regular force is supplemented by the "police reserve," which is made up of some 17,000 former members of the police force, and an additional 19,000 volunteer civilians organized into a "reserve police force." This civilian force was established in 1961 following widespread unrest in the country, and its task is to assist the SAP when additional manpower is required.

As growing numbers of South Africans have taken to the streets to express their grievances, the police have responded with a vengeance. Equipped with helicopters, armored vehicles, metal-tipped whips, tear gas, rubber bullets, birdshot and buckshot, paramilitary police units have not hesitated to direct the full force of their arsenal against protestors. Together with the military troops, the police have killed some two-thirds of the 1400 people who have lost their lives during the unrest.

On many occasions, the police have responded to protest actions by resorting in the first instance to lethal weapons. Pursuant to the criminal and security legislation, police making arrests or responsible for crowd control are supposed to use live ammunition only as a matter of last resort. Nevertheless, a judicial commission of inquiry into the deaths of 20 people in Langa on March 21, 1985, when police opened fire on a funeral procession, found that on that occasion the police were equipped only with rifles, heavy shotgun cartridges and pistols, and had not even been issued non-lethal riot control weapons. In other incidents of unrest, where such non-lethal weapons have been available, reports indicate that live ammunition is also frequently employed.

The excessive brutality of the police and their central function within the State's apparatus of repression have resulted in some violent attacks against them by several township residents during the unrest. Black policemen who live in the townships have been singled out in particular, and a number have been killed in these attacks.

C. The South African Defense Force

Like the police, South Africa's armed forces have played a central role in maintaining the system of apartheid. The military has been called upon to play an increasing role in suppressing internal disorder, most notably in the townships where the armed forces have been deployed during the current unrest. This function has given the South African Defense Force (SADF), which comprises the army, air force, navy and Directorate of Military Intelligence, unprecedented influence over internal affairs.

In the past ten years, the SADF has evolved from a conventional force oriented primarily toward external defense to a principal force in the internal security structure, with increasing influence over domestic government policy. Military commanders are believed to dominate the State Security Council. The current Minister of Defense, General Magnus Malan, who sits on the SSC, is a former Chief of the SADF and was the first serving officer to be appointed to the Cabinet in the history of the Republic.

The SADF, which is headed by General Johan Geldenhuys, consists of a regular trained permanent force of some 83,400 men and women, but its largest component by far is made up of conscripts who serve full time for a period of two years. National service is compulsory only for white males, but conscription for Coloreds and Indians has been under active discussion since the new Constitution was implemented. After their full-time service, the men must join an active reserve known as the Citizen Force, in which they must serve for 720 days over a period of 12 years. After this, they are assigned to local militia groups known as Commandos, and may spend up to 12 days each year at army camps up to the age of 55. There are a few black units in the permanent Defense Force but, in contrast to the SAP, the SADF is overwhelmingly white.

The SADF first began to assume a major role in the current unrest in October 1984, when the government announced that SADF units would be increasingly used in the townships to assist the police. On October 23, 1984, a combined force of police and army personnel, some 7000-strong, was deployed in a massive security operation in the townships of Sebokeng, Sharpeville and Boipatong. The townships were sealed off and, in a sweeping house-to-house search, the majority of all males in the townships -- including children -- were arrested and taken to the sports stadium for processing. In Sebokeng alone, some 400 people were detained as a result of this operation. Defending the decision to bring in troops, the Minister of Law and Order,

Louis Le Grange, declared that the SADF would thereafter be deployed "in all other circumstances that we may decide." Since then, the SADF has been routinely deployed in the troubled townships to carry out all manner of policing operations.

An amendment to the Defense Act,[8] effective July 18, 1984, clarified the conditions under which the SADF could be used to carry out internal police functions in South Africa. The amendment, which was prompted by criticism that the SADF was being used to implement the policy of apartheid, provides that the SADF is to assist the police in defending the country, preventing or suppressing terrorism or internal disorder, and preserving life, health, property and the maintenance of essential services.

During the State of Emergency, soldiers of all ranks were granted the same far-reaching powers as were the police (see Section F, *infra*). There have been numerous reports of violent and abusive behavior by soldiers in the townships, often toward children. Some soldiers have carried out extra-judicial detentions, holding children in army camps or armoured vehicles and physically assaulting and abusing them (see Chapter IV, *infra*). One 14 year-old boy, for example, was held with several other youths in an army camp outside Daveyton for eight days in September 1985, during which he was deprived of food and subjected to severe physical abuse, including the administering of electric shocks to his hands, intensified by the simultaneous application of water. Less sophisticated than the security police in the use of such methods of torture, his captors have left him with burned and blackened scars.

Both the State President and the Minister of Law and Order have recently declared their intention to employ even greater forces in the townships if necessary.

----

8. Act No. 44 of 1957, Section 3.

D. Security Legislation

The state's security legislation, consolidated in the Internal Security Act (ISA) of 1982,[9] establishes wide-ranging state authority to control and suppress all manner of opposition and dissent. The Act defines offenses against state security, such as terrorism, sabotage and subversion, very broadly. These offenses carry heavy prison sentences upon conviction.

The Act also provides for the indefinite *incommunicado* detention without charge of persons for security reasons.[10] The Minister of Law and Order can order the detention of anyone considered likely to commit such offenses or otherwise to endanger state security.[11] Such detention is also authorized for the purpose of interrogating suspects about such activities.[12] Potential witnesses in a security trial can be detained for the entire length of the proceedings.[13]

The ISA authorizes another measure of control that is as perverse as it is dehumanizing: persons said to be engaging in or promoting activities that endanger state security or public order -- or simply thought likely to do so -- can be "banned." Banning orders typically restrict the subject's movement and activities, prohibit him or her from being publicly quoted, and forbid him or her to meet with more than one person at a time and to join certain organizations or serve on public bodies.[14]

----

9. Act No. 74 of 1982. Enforcement of this law falls within the ambit of the Directorate of Security Legislation of the Department of Justice. The Director of this body is also responsible to the Minister of Law and Order, who controls the police and is responsible for the implementation of much of the ISA. Both the Ministers of Justice and Law and Order also sit on the State Security Council.

10. See Chapter VI.A., infra.

11. Act No. 74 of 1982, Section 28.

12. Id., Section 29.

13. Id., Section 31.

14. Id., Sections 18-21.

Persons who are banned, held in preventive detention, or convicted of a security offense may also be subjected thereafter to a variety of civil restrictions. They may, for example, be forbidden to practice law or serve as a member of Parliament.

Organizations can also be banned. The ISA provides for organizations to be declared unlawful if they threaten state security or public order.[15] Pursuant to this provision, the high school students' organization COSAS[16] was banned in August last year. Accordingly, it is now an offense to be a member of COSAS, to display or possess anything indicating a prior association with it, to take part in any of its former activities, or to advocate or encourage the achievement of any of its objectives. Similarly, publications may also be banned if they are believed to threaten state security or public order.

Still another provision of the ISA empowers the Minister of Law and Order or a magistrate to ban or impose restrictions on all manner of gatherings and meetings.[17] This provision has been widely used throughout the unrest to suppress all kinds of political activity and organization. A ban on all outdoor meetings, renewed annually, has been in effect since 1976, and was again renewed in 1986. Blanket bans have been imposed for varying periods on all meetings of certain organizations. At times, the government has banned all meetings with a particular object or in a particular area, and a number of specific bans on individual meetings have also been imposed. In September 1984, for example, a ban was imposed on all gatherings in the Pretoria-Witwatersrand-Vereeniging area at which any government action or policy was to be attacked, criticized, discussed or even approved and defended.

The United Democratic Front, a multi-racial, non-parliamentary opposition coalition, and its affiliates have been the frequent targets of bans on meetings, although the

----

15. Id., Sections 4 and 5.

16. See Chapter I, supra.

17. Id., Section 46.

organization itself has not so far been declared unlawful. Meetings of youth organizations have also been singled out for banning. On June 28, 1985, out of 37 organizations whose meetings were banned by the Minister of Law and Order, 23 were youth organizations, including COSAS.[18]

Township funerals for victims of the unrest have become practically the only opportunity for blacks lawfully to gather together, and are frequently the occasion for voicing opposition to the government. Many of these funerals have been banned or restricted pursuant to the ISA, often at the last minute, resulting in bitter confrontations with police and further outbreaks of violence.[19]

The ISA also accords the police far-reaching authority to use force in dealing with perceived threats to public safety. Specifically, police have the power to disperse prohibited gatherings as well as lawful gatherings that seriously threaten life or valuable property, using such force as may be "necessary," including firearms and lethal weapons if other means have failed.[20] The police can also arrest and detain without a warrant for 48 hours anyone whom they believe to be contributing to a state of public disturbance or disorder. Such persons can be detained without charge for a further 14 days on a warrant issued by a magistrate.[21]

E. Other Permanent Legislation

In addition to the security legislation, various other statutes provide alternative means of control. For example, the defense legislation[22] authorizes censorship and the

----

18. Notice No. 1433, Government Gazette No. 9806, June 28, 1985.

19. Additional restrictions were also placed on all funerals during the State of Emergency.

20. Act No. 74 of 1982, Section 49.

21. Id., Section 50.

22. Defense Act, No. 44 of 1957.

prohibition of access to designated areas and various other means of control to prevent "internal disorder," simply by declaring an area to be "operational." Also, a variety of provisions in ordinary criminal statutes have been widely invoked during the unrest. The Intimidation Act[23] makes it a criminal offense to intimidate anyone by threats or violence. A number of people have been charged with this during the unrest, particularly those organizing protest activities such as strikes and boycotts. Thousands of people have been charged with the common law crime of public violence and related criminal offenses, such as arson, trespass and malicious damage to property.[24]

Public scrutiny and criticism of the activities of the security forces, particularly in relation to detainees, are severely hampered by various acts that restrict the publication of information. Section 44(1)(f) of the Prisons Act[25] makes it a crime to publish "false" information about the experience of a prisoner or ex-prisoner without taking "reasonable steps" to verify that it is correct. Similarly, publishing "false" information about police conduct without reasonable grounds to believe it is true is a criminal offense (with the accused bearing the onus of proof) pursuant to Section 27(b) of the Police Act.[26] Section 4 of the Protection of Information Act[27] prohibits the publication of any information prejudicial to state security under penalty of ten years' imprisonment or a fine of R10,000.

In short, the extremely broad and far-reaching provisions of the ordinary security legislation, supplemented by various other statutes, permit the state and the security forces to maintain tight control in the townships. Nevertheless, when the State of Emergency was declared in

----

23. Act No. 72 of 1982.

24. See Chapter VI.B., infra.

25. Act No. 8 of 1959.

26. Act No. 7 of 1958. Regulations in effect during the State of Emergency made it an offense to publish the name or identity of an emergency detainee until the detention had been officially confirmed by the police.

27. Act No. 84 of 1982.

July last year, the security forces were given additional powers of control. It is widely believed that the primary motive of the State President in declaring an Emergency after almost a year of bitter civil unrest was to silence South Africa's critics and to permit the drastic and severe enforcement of its repressive powers behind the shield of an extraordinary situation that, the government argued, justified a draconian response.

F. The State of Emergency

On July 21, 1985 the State President imposed a State of Emergency in 36 magisterial districts.[28] The declaration, made pursuant to Section 2(1) of the Public Safety Act,[29] stated that circumstances had arisen that seriously threatened public order and safety and could not be adequately dealt with under the ordinary law of the land.[30] The magisterial districts affected by the Emergency were located mainly in the urban townships of the Transvaal and Eastern Cape. In the months that followed, the Emergency was lifted in a few of these districts but was extended to others, most significantly to eight districts in the Western Cape on October 26, 1985.[31]

Emergency regulations were promulgated by the State President without any debate or authorization by Parliament, which was not then in session. These regulations significantly extended the powers of the ordinary security forces to take measures which, under the ISA, would have required the authorization of a Cabinet minister, a magistrate or a higher-ranking police officer.

----

28. Proclamation R.120, Government Gazette, No. 9876, July 21, 1985.

29. Act No. 3 of 1953

30. The last time a State of Emergency was declared in South Africa was in 1960 in the wake of the Sharpeville massacre, in which 69 people were killed by the security forces.

31. Proclamation R.200, Government Gazette, No. 9992, October 26, 1985.

Under the regulations, any member of the security forces (of whatever rank) could make arrests without a warrant.[32] For purposes of the Emergency, the security forces were defined to include the SADF, the police, the railways police and the prison service. Those who were arrested could be detained without charge for 14 days and, on the order of the Minister of Law and Order, indefinitely thereafter as long as the Emergency remained in effect. More than 7900 people were detained under these provisions, some for the entire eight months' duration of the Emergency.

Special rules and regulations, including a strict disciplinary code, were brought into force in respect of emergency detainees that were even harsher than the detention provisions of the ISA. The emergency detainees were denied even the few meagre rights accorded to detainees held under the ISA, such as the right to make representations concerning their detention; the right to a periodic review of their cases; and, for those held for interrogation, the right to visits by an inspector and a magistrate.

Section 2 of the emergency regulations enabled any member of the security forces to order people to disperse, using such force as was deemed necessary, if their conduct might endanger public safety and order or life and property. This enabled security forces to break up all kinds of gatherings, regardless of whether they had been specifically prohibited by the ISA, and to disperse groups at will. In addition, the Police Commissioner or anyone acting on his authority could, under Section 6 of the regulations, issue wide-ranging orders to seal off the townships, control essential services, close down businesses, impose curfews and censor news reports of the unrest. Failure to comply with an order or regulation carried a penalty of 10 years' imprisonment or a fine of R20,000 (about $10,000).

During the State of Emergency additional regulations and orders were imposed to restrict media coverage of the unrest, to curb school boycotts and to restrict the holding of funerals. A new form of banning order was introduced

----

32. See Chapter VI.C., infra.

against a number of emergency detainees upon their release. These orders typically imposed severe restrictions on the person's movement, activities, utterances, attendance at meetings or educational institutions and participation in certain organizations. At least 59 people were banned in this way during the Emergency, whereas only 10 persons were banned in 1985 pursuant to the ISA banning provisions.

The emergency regulations effectively prevented any recourse to the courts. They provided a blanket prospective indemnity against any legal proceedings relating to all conduct performed in "good faith" in connection with the Emergency. The indemnity extended not only to the security forces, but also to the State President, the Cabinet and any employee of the state or anyone acting on the authority of such persons. It was explicitly provided that "good faith" for the purposes of this indemnity was to be presumed until the contrary was proved. Furthermore, no court could set aside or issue a stay of any order or notice issued under the emergency regulations. On October 26, 1985 this indemnity provision was extended to cover the actions of the security forces in areas of the country not subject to the State of Emergency.[33]

The broad powers granted to the security forces, coupled with their indemnity against legal proceedings and the sweeping restrictions introduced in November 1985 on press reporting of their activities,[34] granted them a license to act without sanction or restraint during the Emergency. This resulted in an increase in violence and in widespread allegations of security force abuses of detainees and township residents.

The State of Emergency was lifted on March 7, 1986 but there is no reason to believe that this will result in a significant moderation of the activities of the security forces. The State President has made it clear that some of the emergency powers will now be incorporated into the ordinary security legislation. Since the Emergency was

----

33. Proclamation R201, Government Gazette No. 9993, October 26, 1985.

34. Proclamation R208, Government Gazette, No. 10004, November 2, 1985.

lifted, more than 100 people have been killed in outbreaks of unrest, bringing the daily death toll to an average of five per day, compared with less than four during the Emergency.[35]

----

35. The pre-Emergency average daily death toll was 1.67, rising to 3.66 during the Emergency.

CHAPTER III

Violence in the Streets

Since the unrest began, the South African government has made it clear that it is determined to suppress it primarily by the use of force. Cloaked with impunity and armed for battle, military troops have transformed some townships into virtual war zones. Their conduct in quelling the unrest has been characterized by an unprecedented level of violence and brutality.

A particularly tragic dimension of the violence has been its claim on the lives of South Africa's children. Many have been killed; still more have been injured and terrorized in a conflict that is being waged with lethal weapons.

Far from being spared the brunt of state-sanctioned violence, children often have been its special target. At times, violence against children has been the result of a deliberate strategy of the security forces to suppress student organizations and protests. In their frequent sweeps and patrols through the townships, security forces have singled out young people of school-age for arrest, pursuing them with sjamboks -- metal-tipped whips -- and shooting at random at any child who runs away.

Schools have become battle grounds as the security forces have attempted to put an end to the widespread school boycotts. Many pupils, including those not participating in the boycotts, have been arrested, injured and even killed in these attacks.

In other cases, children have been the unfortunate victims, caught in the perpetual cross-fire of the confrontations in areas where they live, play, go to school, attend church or run errands. Play areas in the townships are practically non-existent and children often play in the streets, making them vulnerable targets for random arrest, assault and the cross-fire of bullets and shot. Young children who, out of natural curiosity, have been drawn to watch burning barricades or other incidents of unrest, have been pursued by the police or soldiers, assaulted and sometimes arrested and accused of being the perpetrators of the incident.

The pervasive and indiscriminate nature of policing operations in the townships has made it virtually inevitable that innocent children would fall within their sweep. In many townships armed police and army units conduct frequent patrols on foot and in the heavy armored vehicles known as "casspirs" and "hippos." One young girl in Cape Town told the Lawyers Committee, "We have had to learn to recognize the different uniforms and vehicles of the security forces. Even the little children now know which units shoot to kill."[36]

Roadblocks, house-to-house searches, curfews, the immediate dispersal of any group or gathering by force, as well as widespread arrests and detentions are common features of daily life for many black people. Tear gas, rubber bullets, birdshot, buckshot, whips and even live ammunition are routinely and indiscriminately used by the security forces in these policing operations, all too often with tragic consequences for children and other residents.[37] Furthermore, weapons such as tear gas, birdshot and rubber bullets that are intended for riot control and are supposedly non-lethal can have fatal consequences when used against children, especially the very young.

A. Children Killed

At least 201 children have been killed by the police in unrest incidents during 1985, according to the latest

----

36. Interview by Helena Cook, Cape Town, November 16, 1985.

37. A report by the Southern African Catholic Bishops' Conference published in November 1984, compiled from sworn affidavits collected in various townships, details wide-ranging police brutality, including the indiscriminate use of fire-arms and tear gas, excessive beatings and other assaults, provocative, abusive and humiliating conduct, insensitivity and violence against mourners at funerals, wanton property damage and allegations of rape of two young girls by white policemen. Report on Police Conduct during Township Protests August-November 1984 S.A.C.B.C., November 1984.

government statistics.[38] All of these children were black. A survey of 77 of these deaths conducted in November 1985 revealed that 44 of the children were shot dead, 17 were burned to death, three were run over by police vehicles, four were drowned while fleeing from police, two were beaten to death, one was stabbed and six died of "unknown causes." Nineteen of the victims in this November survey were under ten years old.[39]

One victim was four year-old Mitah Ngobeni, shot dead on September 10, 1985 by a rubber bullet while playing in the yard of her home in Atteridgeville. Although rubber bullets are supposed to be non-lethal, Mitah died of skull and brain damage and excessive blood loss, according to the findings at the inquest.

Constable Albert Fourie, the police officer who killed Mitah, alleged that a group was throwing stones at his vehicle, and he fired because he believed that his life was in danger. He is reported to have said at the inquest, "Shooting was my only option." Constable Neville Graham, who was with Fourie at the time, said he believed the latter had acted reasonably. The head of Fourie's patrol agreed, saying, "tear gas and sjamboks, for example, were impractical in this case. Violence can spread incredibly quickly." Yet a student who witnessed the shooting testified in court that he had not seen anyone throwing stones. He said he saw the police car draw level with Mitah's house and then heard shots. Nevertheless, the magistrate at the inquest found that no one could be held responsible for the child's death.[40]

One month later, another Atteridgeville child was beaten to death by police. A white police constable, Daniel Johannes Blom, has been charged with culpable homicide after the death of 13 year-old Moses Mope, who was attacked as he was on his way to church with friends on

----

38. Reply to Parliamentary Question, March 3, 1985. These figures appear to refer only to police action and do not include SADF action.

39. Source: International Defense and Aid Fund for Southern Africa.

40. "Mitah's death: nobody blamed," The Star, November 27, 1985; "A'Ville death: nobody blamed," Pretoria News, November 27, 1985; "Constable says he feared for his life," The Star, November 26, 1985.

October 21, 1985. According to witnesses, a private car had pulled up beside the group and the children fled. One of the men in the car, recognized by witnesses to be a policeman, caught Moses, brutally assaulted him and trampled on him. A neighbor took Moses home, covered with blood. "When I touched his stomach he pulled away in agony," his father is reported to have said. "I also noticed his jaw was cracked and he was injured on the head and other parts of the body." Moses was only semi-conscious and died on the way to the hospital.[41]

In November 1985, the unrest monitoring group set up by the Parliamentary opposition group, the Progressive Federalist Party, heard testimony from a resident of Crossroads, outside Cape Town, who had witnessed the deliberate shooting of 15 year-old Dominic Ntlemenza:

> This boy was walking and then I saw the casspir come down the road. One policeman jumped off the casspir and shot the boy. The boy tried to stand up and then they shot him in the head.
>
> Then they went away and they left the body there. There were no boys throwing stones next to the road. The boy, whose name I now know was Dominic, was alone.

Dominic's mother only found out that her son was dead when his body was found the next day, left at the side of the road.[42]

Parents whose children do not return home must face the terrible uncertainty of not knowing whether the child has been arrested, has been hospitalized with injuries, or is already dead. Sixteen year-old Oscar left his house on the evening of October 5, 1985 to go to the movies. It was not until 6 a.m. the next morning that his father learned that Oscar had stopped at a house where a wedding was being held and that a policeman had opened fire on the guests.

----

41. "Slain boy: Constable charged," Sowetan, November 21, 1985.

42. "Man says police shot boy in head," Natal Mercury, November 7, 1985.

The father went to the scene of the shooting, where he learned that his son was already dead. Based on information furnished by witnesses, Oscar's father stated: "All the guests apparently scattered and ran for cover. My son was hit in the back. I am told that he fell face down and the policeman came over and kicked the body until it turned over." He added: "My son was buried on October 12th. At an all night vigil that was held on October 11 for him, the police came and fired at my house in the early hours of the morning and another child was killed."[43]

A mother in Crossroads last saw her 13 year-old son alive when he left the house at 4:30 p.m. on October 7, 1985. It took days of searching before she found her son, whose body she traced to the state mortuary. He had been shot by the police but no one had contacted her or her husband. She was unable to learn the circumstances of the shooting, but was horrified that the mortuary refused to hand over her son's clothing because "it was too full of holes."[44]

When violence erupted in the Western Cape in August and September last year, many children were among its victims. The security forces typically open fire on crowds as a means to disperse them. On September 18, 1985 a ten year-old girl was shot dead when police fired on a crowd allegedly throwing stones.[45]

Outside Cape Town, 16 year-old Botoman Mtuze was shot dead on August 28, 1985 when police clashed with thousands of demonstrators planning a peaceful march to Pollsmoor Prison to call for the release of jailed African National Congress leader Nelson Mandela.[46] The brutality of the police against the marchers provoked further outbreaks of protest and led to more violence. The official police list of 24 victims killed during the ten days following

----

43. Statement, Johannesburg, November 1985.

44. Statement, Cape Town, November 8, 1985.

45. "Girl, 10, one of three killed on Cape Flats" Argus, September 8, 1985.

46. "In Cape Town, a Fallen Youth is Mourned, and Anger Rises," New York Times, September 14, 1985.

the attempted march included nine children aged from 12 to 17 years.[47]

Three students, including a teenage boy, were shot dead by police on March, 1986 as they waited with a large crowd of school children outside a White River magistrates' court, where a number of their fellow pupils were appearing on charges of public violence. More than one hundred others were injured when police suddenly opened fire to disperse the crowd. The attorney representing the accused had attempted to negotiate with the police to allow six of the students to enter the court room as representatives of the others, who could not all be accomodated inside the building. The police opened fire without warning or provocation, according to eyewitnesses. The shocked attorney made a statement about the incident with the consent of the Johannesburg Bar Council. He said afterwards:

> I feel it is my duty to make the following observations: The crowd was not uncontrollable. I heard no order to disperse. I neither saw nor experienced any tear gas being fired. I saw nothing to justify the view that shooting was the last resort available to the police.[48]

A number of children have died from the effects of tear gas. Tear gas is routinely used by the security forces to break up gatherings of all kinds. There are numerous reports of police releasing tear gas into churches, meetings halls and even private houses to disperse a crowd or merely to force those inside to come out. The gas can be lethal, especially if there is prolonged or excessive exposure to it, such as when it is used in enclosed spaces. Infants and very young children who are unable to escape from closed areas where the gas is released are particularly at risk.

----

47. "SAP list of dead," Cape Times, September 7, 1985.

48. "A Few Minutes at White River" and "The Moderate Man who Refused to Stay Silent," Weekly Mail, March 21-27, 1986.

Two babies were killed by tear gas in Mamelodi township, just outside Pretoria, on November 21, 1985. On that day, women were marching to present the mayor with a list of grievances that included the continued presence of SADF troops in the township and severe restrictions imposed by a magistrate on the holding of funerals. At least 19 died as a result of police actions to disperse the women.[49] Witnesses reported to the Lawyers Committee that, as people attempted to flee from the barrage of tear gas, birdshot, rubber bullets and live ammunition, police pursued them. Tear gas was fired into a number of houses to "flush people out," and the two babies later died in the hospital from the effects of the gas.

One eyewitness who was at the march took refuge in the house where one of the babies died. She told the Lawyers Committee:

> Tear gas was fired directly inside the house and everyone had to hold a wet cloth over their face. The mother, Phephi, had a small baby only a few months old. The baby was badly affected by the gas and her eyes were streaming. The next day I heard that the baby had died . . . . [50]

Police countered that one of the babies, Trocia Ndlovu, had died from malnourishment and diarrhea. Trocia's mother, testifying before a commission of inquiry set up by the Pretoria Council of Churches in February, rejected this explanation, and insisted that her daughter was perfectly healthy before she inhaled the tear gas fumes from a cannister thrown directly at the house.

On January 6, 1986, in Walmer township just outside Port Elizabeth, a 13 year-old girl died from a head wound inflicted by a tear gas cannister fired by police when they attempted to disperse a crowd at a student rally. The child,

----

49. For a detailed account of this incident, see Mamelodi - South Africa's Response to Peaceful Protest, Lawyers Committee for Human Rights, January 1986.

50. Interview by Helena Cook, Pretoria, November 27, 1985.

Ntombekhaya Mgubase, was on a shopping errand when she was hit by the cannister that fractured her skull.[51]

B. Children Injured by Police Action

Numerous children have been injured by the indiscriminate firing of birdshot, buckshot and sometimes live ammunition in operations by the security forces to disperse crowds, or after incidents of violence or property damage in the townships. Birdshot and buckshot are often used when people are running away from the police to prevent them from escaping.

Like tear gas, birdshot and buckshot are supposed to be non-lethal weapons but can cause very serious injuries or even death, especially in the case of children. Fourteen year-old Ernest was shot by the police on October 25, 1985 while visiting his aunts in Meadowlands. He was standing in the yard when a police car drove past and police in plainclothes shot at him. He was hit in the spinal cord, and is now permanently paralyzed from the waist down.[52]

In January 1986, a Cape Town hospital confirmed that three school children had been admitted who had been paralyzed by gunshot wounds. The youngest was 12 years old. The mother of one of the boys stated that they had been shot by police.[53]

Children who are out on the streets when a confrontation with police occurs are often caught in the cross fire or deliberately shot at. Eleven year-old Peter spent four days in the hospital after he was shot on June 16, 1985 as he was walking to his sister's house:

----

51. "Tearsmoke bullet caused girl's death," Eastern Province Herald, January 13, 1986.

52. Statement, Johannesburg, February 2, 1986.

53. "Three kids paralyzed," City Press, January 19, 1986.

I was walking along M. street when I heard
people chanting. I was approximately 30m
away from the crowd. I heard some shots,
turned around and ran. I was shot and fell
down. I tried to crawl away, two people
unknown to me picked me up and took me to
G's place. From there I was taken to
Vryburg hospital.[54]

A young boy in Port Alfred was brutally beaten by
police when they burst into a house in pursuit of rioters.
The terrified child was hiding under a pillow. When the
police found him they dragged him outside and beat him,
only releasing him when he pleaded that he was merely ten
years old.[55]

The violence directed at children causes particular
anguish to their families, who are often helpless when
confronted with armed soldiers or police. In one extreme
case in Port Elizabeth, a father was allegedly shot dead by
the security forces as he tried to restrain them from hurting
his daughter.[56]

Part of the pattern of violence by the security forces
includes general and often severe assault of young people
picked up by police but not formally arrested. Children
who run away when they see police vehicles, as most do, are
at particular risk of being pursued and caught, after which
they are brutally assaulted and simply left on the streets.

Thirteen year-old Sipho was walking home from the
shops on September 30, 1985 when he noticed the police
chasing some boys. Not wanting to get caught up in the
chase, he ran into a nearby house to hide. When they saw
Sipho run away, the police followed him and put him in
their van, where they beat him. According to a statement
taken by the unrest monitoring group of the Progressive
Federalist Party:

----

54. Statement, Johannesburg, 1985.

55. Affidavit, Port Alfred, November 10, 1984.

56. The Children's Emergency, Black Sash report, March 1986.

In the van the police beat Sipho, kicking him
with their boots on the legs and in the
stomach while Sipho was half lying on the
bench inside the van. The police also beat
Sipho on the front of the body with
sjamboks. One of the policemen squeezed
him round the neck as if to strangle Sipho.
A sjambok was also used to pull Sipho's head
back by pulling it across his open mouth.[57]

The police later pushed Sipho out of the van some
distance from his home. A woman who found him took him
back to his house. By the time his mother returned, Sipho
was in serious condition, and was taken immediately by
ambulance to the hospital, where he underwent surgery.

On October 3, 1985 another 15 year-old boy in
Nyanga was picked up at the place where he was working
when the police came by chasing some other boys. The
police asked him where the boys were, and when he could
not answer they lashed him with a sjambok and put him
into their van. Inside the van

the police closed all the windows and put on
teargas masks. They shot off a teargas
cannister while they were hitting him. They
also made him drink some foul tasting liquid
which is presumed to be urine from a small
plastic juice bottle.[58]

When some local residents approached the police to
ask what they were doing, tear gas was thrown at them and
the police threatened them with a gun. Later, the child was
released at the soccer stadium. Before he returned home,
some police went to his house, apparently looking for him.
They threatened his mother with a gun and took cigarettes
and R200 from the house before leaving. When the boy's
mother went to the police station to make a complaint, she
was told to go away.

----

57. Statement, Cape Town, October 1985.

58. Statement, Cape Town, October 4, 1985.

Michael, who is only nine years old, went with some friends, the oldest of whom was only 12, to look at a van that had been set alight near his house. As they walked home an armored vehicle came around the corner. The children were scared and began to run. As they fled, the soldiers shot at them. Michael was shot in both legs and ran into a neighbor's yard. The soldiers followed him, hit him and asked why he had run away. They smelled his hands for petrol and accused him of burning the van. Eventually they left, and only then was Michael taken to a clinic for treatment.[59]

In one case, a young boy who fled when he saw the police chasing a group of other children was shot even though he had fallen to the ground. Doctors in a clinic in Crossroads treated the 12 year-old boy for gunshot wounds in October 1985. From the way the bullets had entered the boy's body, the doctors concluded that he could not have been running away but must have been lying down. The child said he was on an errand for his parents when he met a group of boys running from the police. He had tried to run also but fell while trying to climb a wall, after which police came and shot him in both thighs. He was later charged with public violence by the police.[60]

In many instances, the confrontation that spills over to mere bystanders is provoked by nothing more menacing than a family celebration. Zwakhe, aged four years, was shot as he was standing with his parents on a street corner near his house. A wedding was in progess nearby and the exuberant crowd attracted the attention of a policeman, who apparently opened fire at random, now a typical police response to the sight of any crowd. Zwakhe's mother told the Lawyers Committee:

> My husband was shot with birdshot in both legs. I was shot in my leg and my right breast. My son was shot in the foot, the thigh and in his forehead. I lost consciousness. I was eight months pregnant

----

59. Statement, Johannesburg, September 18, 1985.

60. "Doctors Say Child Shot Lying Down," Weekly Mail, October 25, 1985.

at the time. The policeman came and apologized. He said he would "stand for everything." We went to the hospital. My son has had to go to the hospital three times. They cannot take out the stitches in his forehead because the wound is septic.

Instead of some form of redress as the policeman had promised, two days later two policemen came to the house and threatened to charge the parents with the crime of public violence. Mrs. M, who gave birth to her baby prematurely shortly after this incident, said: "My son Zwakhe is now very frightened and refuses to play outside the house anymore."[61]

In many cases, security force violence has been purely gratuitous. There are numerous reports of the police and army taking shots at people for no particular reason while on routine patrol. A father in Langa described how he was sitting at home with his family on September 11, 1985 when "a casspir happened to pass by and shot birdshot through the window pane." His two young children, aged nine and ten years, were both shot. The younger child was shot just below his eye and spent nine days in the hospital. The father said that only one shot was fired and that there had been no trouble in the vicinity at the time. He is convinced that "there was no reason at all to shoot my house."[62]

A number of reports concerning police and army conduct suggest that some resort to violence simply for sport. On February 3, 1985 in Cradock, two policemen grabbed a 16 year-old boy as he was fetching laundry, and dragged him into the street. According to the youth, they "pushed me and told me to run." As he ran, the police shot at him, wounding him in the buttocks and the back of both legs, causing him to fall. When a hippo appeared, "the same two policemen picked me up by my legs and threw me into the hippo." The boy was unable to walk and was taken to

----

61. Interview by Helena Cook, Johannesburg, November 21, 1985.

62. Affidavit, Cape Town, September 24, 1985.

the hospital, where he was kept under 24-hour armed police guard, accused of being a ringleader in the township.[63]

Chantal is 17 years old. She was arrested in Cape Town on September 24, 1985, after being stopped at a roadblock. She believes she was singled out because she is a member of the Student Representative Council at her school. She described how she was humiliated during interrogation at the police station. Ten male policemen and one female were present:

> [A policeman] smacked me from behind on the rear right hand side of my neck. I grabbed hold of the desk to prevent me from falling over. Everybody laughed about what had happened while the questioning continued . . . The short man smacked me on my right ear so that I almost fell to the ground and another "white" man smacked me on the left hand side of my face . . . . [T]he short man put both his hands round my throat and lifted me off the ground. He choked me in that position (i.e. feet off the floor) for about two minutes whereafter he threw me to the ground. I fell on my back. The rest of the people all cheered and laughed and one of the men hugged the short [policeman]. . . . [Two others] then pulled me by my hair about 5 times while I was questioned and while answering. . . . A tall man was hitting continuously, hitting me with his fists on my back. . . . [The short policeman] then smacked me against my right ear again. I was then feeling dizzy, my ear was "singing." . . . The short man then hit me with his fist in my right eye. Everyone was then laughing and enjoying themselves. I told the person who was questioning me to tell them to stop hitting me because I thought that they were going to kill me . . . . [64]

----

63. Affidavit, Cradock, February 5, 1985.

64. Affidavit, Cape Town, September 27, 1985.

A report prepared by the Southern African Catholic Bishops' Conference (SACBC) describes a number of humiliations perpetrated on township residents, including verbal abuse, cutting hair with knives and ordering people to strip naked before beating them. The report concluded that "some of the police regarded their duties as a kind of sport."[65]

C. Arrests of Hospitalized Children

Children who are shot face the risk of arrest if they seek medical treatment. From the early days of the unrest, the security forces have maintained an armed guard at some of the hospitals and clinics, routinely arresting anyone with birdshot or buckshot wounds, regardless of how the injuries were sustained. The mere fact of the injury appears to be sufficient for the police to allege involvement in unrest incidents. As a result, although swift medical treatment may be vital for the child's very survival after being shot, many parents are now afraid to take their injured children to hospitals for treatment.

Miriam, who is 12 years old, was shot on June 17, 1985 as she was returning from a shop with a loaf of bread. She saw a large group of boys and girls running in all directions. One of the girls told Miriam to run because the police were coming. She could not keep up with the others, and was left behind:

> I saw a white policeman come out of a house
> I was running past. He had a long gun . . . .
> I was alone in the street and ran faster, still
> holding the bread. I did not hear any call
> from the policeman.
>
> As I reached the corner of 5th Avenue, I
> heard one bang and felt a terrible pain in my
> lower back. I fell. I was in terrible pain, but

----

65. Report on Police Conduct during Township Protests August-November 1984 S.A.C.B.C., November 1984.

conscious. I felt where the pain was in my
back and saw that my hand was bloody.[66]

The policeman did not pursue Miriam after she was shot.
People from a nearby house took her in and called her
father, who took her to the hospital. Once at the hospital,
however, Miriam was formally arrested and kept under
police guard.

After a month in the hospital the police moved
Miriam to the police station and then to prison, where she
was held for four days before appearing in court on a
charge of public violence, allegedly for stone throwing.
Miriam told the police that she had not thrown any stones.
At her trial she was still very weak, and did not give
evidence, having no legal representation. The magistrate
sentenced this 12 year-old girl to five years' suspended
imprisonment.[67]

Throughout the ordeal, Miriam bore a bullet in her
lower back, as she will for the rest of her life. She explains:
"The doctor said I may be paralyzed if they remove it."[68]

Sixteen year-old Zisamile Mapela died in Soweto on
August 3, 1985 from shot wounds. Police fired after a stone
was thrown at their armored vehicle, and Zisamile was hit.
His father did not dare to take his son to the hospital
because he feared Zisamile would be arrested. A local
doctor stitched the wound but could not remove the bullet.
The next day the boy's eyes seemed strange and he
complained of feeling unwell. Hours later, he was dead.[69]

A doctor at a hospital in the Eastern Cape described
to the Lawyers Committee how he had tried to safeguard the
patients brought to him with shot wounds and other unrest-

----

66. Statement, Bhongolethu, December 28, 1985.

67. Id.

68. Id.

69. "Black Mourners Defy South Africa on Funeral Rule," New York Times,
    August 4, 1985.

- 43 -

related injuries by keeping records that did not reveal the exact nature of their injuries. Even then it was difficult to avoid the police who routinely patrolled the hospital:

> Police would walk in at any time through Casualty. At one point they installed a permanent booth outside the entrance to the Casualty Department and the hospital looked more like a military camp with police everywhere. They all carried guns and it created an atmosphere of great fear and tension so that people were afraid to come for help. The nurses were instructed to keep a list of everyone with bullet or shot wounds and a copy of the list went straight to the police. Hospital administrators claimed they were legally bound to do this. This is still going on.

> Once the police arrest someone who requires hospitalization, they keep an armed guard by the bed day and night. Patients are sometimes handcuffed to their beds, even ones who are so sick they could never escape.[70]

According to a statement made by a health spokesman to the Eastern Cape Provincial Council in May last year, 47 patients were held under police or prison guard at eight different hospitals in the Eastern Cape between November 1984 and February 1985. Four of these, aged between 17 and 35, were restricted with leg irons and nine others were handcuffed to their beds. Fifteen of them were aged 18 or younger; the youngest patient under guard was only eight years old.[71]

----

70. Interview by Helena Cook, Port Elizabeth, November 7, 1985.

71. "Handcuffs and leg irons used in E. Cape Hospitals," Cape Times, May 15, 1985.

D. Police Conduct at Funerals

Funerals are frequently the occasion for police harrassment and brutality. Since funerals are now virtually the only legal form of gathering,[72] they have become highly significant occasions for township communities, providing an opportunity for people to come together and express some of their grievances and anger. Funerals of unrest victims are typically attended by thousands of people and often resemble political rallies.

Although the government imposed severe restrictions on funerals of unrest victims shortly after the Emergency was declared,[73] the restrictions were largely ignored by residents. In response, the security forces have taken matters into their own hands, generally harassing mourners and breaking up funeral crowds, usually by force. Children are frequently caught in the midst of these confrontations.

The funeral in Mzinoni township on August 27, 1985 of Mpopi Sam Nhlanhla, who was shot dead by police, became the scene of more violence when police beat and seriously injured scores of young people attending a vigil for the dead boy. According to witnesses, police fired tear gas into the house where the vigil was being held, and began whipping the young people indiscriminately with sjamboks and hitting them with fists. One 15 year-old girl, Somo Vilakazi, said police broke down the door where she was sleeping, assaulted everyone in the house and made them walk to the police station. She claimed that she tried to hide, but a policeman saw her and kicked her in the mouth, as a result of which she lost five teeth. Another young girl, Gugu Shabalala, aged 15, was whipped across the face and

----

72. As previously noted, all outdoor gatherings have been banned by the Minister of Law and Order every year for the past ten years. Since the current period of unrest began, a wide variety of indoor meetings of many organizations also have been banned by the Minister or broken up by police. See Chapter II, supra.

73. Government Notice No. 1746, July 31, 1985. These prohibited all outdoor commemorative services and banned the use of any public address system and the display of banners and placards at the funeral. Only ordained ministers could give public speeches, provided these did not criticize the government. Mourners were required to travel in vehicles along routes pre-determined by the police.

at least ten others sustained eye injuries as a result of the beatings.[74]

Nombulelo, aged 15, was among four busloads of mourners on their way to a funeral in White City on January 4, 1986 when the buses were stopped by police at the entrance to the cemetery:

> A landrover with sneezing gas appeared and released the gas into the buses . . . . [W]e tried to get out of the bus, we then broke windows and went out. We ran to the nearest houses . . . the police then appeared and chased me. He caught me and threw me to the ground and beat me and kicked me.[75]

Petros, aged 15, experienced similar treatment when leaving the cemetery after a funeral on August 31, 1985:

> While the buses were moving towards the Molele home, our bus was stopped by a hippo and policemen boarded it . . . . They asked all the older people to alight and told us they had found petrol bombs and huge rocks on the bus. They started to beat us with their guns, sjamboks and batons. I was injured on the left knee and left knuckle with the butt of a gun . . . . All of us were beaten up including the girls . . . . [W]e were not arrested or charged.[76]

Amos, aged 16, had attended the same funeral. Afterwards he went to the bereaved family's house for the customary refreshments:

> While we were still eating a lot of policemen arrived in hippos and a landrover and started shooting teargas cannisters at us outside in

----

74. "Mourners claim police brutality," The Star, August 28, 1985.

75. Statement, Johannesburg, January, 1986.

76. Statement, Johannesburg, September 2, 1985.

the yard. We ran outside into the street and then I ran to someone's house. I was followed by two black policemen but while I was still outside the yard at the house they started beating me with sjamboks on my legs, my back, my head and through my face . . . . I became unconscious.[77]

Police and army violence at funerals has often resulted in further deaths, perpetuating the cycle of confrontation and violence. In October 1985, 15 year-old Lawrence Cindi was shot dead by police while attending a vigil for a young school friend of his, Mandla Radebe, who had been shot by police some days earlier. A number of Mandla's former school friends, including Lawrence, were in the yard of the Radebe house when three police vehicles drove by. As the children scattered, police fired tear gas and bullets, and fatally shot Lawrence in the head.[78] At a vigil for Lawrence police again arrived to break up the crowd of mourners, brutally whipped them with sjamboks, and arrested many of them.[79]

E. The "Trojan Horse" Incident

An incident in Athlone outside Cape Town on October 15, 1985 provoked special outrage. Known as the "Trojan Horse" incident, it involved a deliberate and wanton ambush by the police.

The atmosphere in the township that day was tense. Some children had been throwing stones and setting up barricades. The police disguised their entry into the township by hiding behind crates in a delivery van, knowing that this would probably provoke more stone throwing in the inflammatory atmosphere. As the van drove in and before residents realized what was happening, the police started

----

77. Statement, Johannesburg, September 2, 1985.

78. "Boy (15) Shot Dead In Soweto," Sowetan, October 23, 1985.

79. Interview by Helena Cook, Johannesburg, November 25, 1985.

shooting wildly from their hidden positions on the truck. In one home alone, one boy was killed and seven others were shot, including three small children. None of these children was involved in the stone throwing. A small boy playing in the street on his bicycle was also shot dead in the surprise attack.

The family from which one of the boys was killed had brought their own four young children and nine others inside the house for safety when the unrest started. One child taking refuge there became very anxious and wanted to return home. Seconds after he opened the door and went outside, followed by four of the other children, the police opened fire, apparently aiming directly at the house. One of the adults in the house told the Lawyers Committee:

> Two seconds after the door opened, the police started shooting. I saw a yellow truck with boxes on it and I realized the police were hiding behind the boxes and shooting. They were aiming straight at the open door. It all happened very quickly. As I tried to shut the door, I was shot in the shoulder.
>
> Two of the younger children were cowering on the bed just inside the door. Andrew (aged 7) was shot in the arm, leg, chest and hip. Thabo (age 10) was shot through his leg and thigh. Michael (16 years) was shot under one arm four times.
>
> Jerry, aged 16, was one of the children who had gone outside. He came crawling back inside on all fours. We didn't realize it then but he had been shot in the head. He staggered into the other room and collapsed on a bed where he died seconds later. A nine year-old child who had been playing in the street on his bicycle was also shot dead.

The witness continued:

> I slammed the door shut but four of police came to the house and kicked it open . . . .

They dragged Jerry's body roughly off the bed and across the floor. They tried to drag another child out too but my mother pleaded with them to wait until his father came . . . . Another child outside who was terrified told the police that I was his mother so that they would let him come inside. They told him that if he came in he must not say anything about what he had seen. Then the police went around the house and picked up all the shot pellets and left.

The police surrounded the house until 2 a.m. the next morning. Three others in the house who had been shot were smuggled out of the back door and taken to a private doctor because the family feared they would be arrested if they left in an ambulance.

The agony of the families whose children were killed was not yet over. They are Muslims and, according to their religious customs, their dead should be buried as soon as possible. When they went to the mortuary to collect Jerry's body, the authorities refused to release it unless the family signed a statement undertaking that no more than 50 people would attend the funeral (in accordance with the emergency regulations). They refused to sign, and several days passed before the body was finally released, only after a massive protest by the community.

The security forces continued to harass the family. Two weeks later, police again stormed into the house without warning as the father and some of his relatives were preparing to go to work. The police threatened to arrest them for "speaking against the government" and to charge them with holding an illegal meeting. On another occasion, the SADF parked a casspir outside the house and walked around in the front yard with rifles cocked.

Two of the children, small girls aged six and nine, now become hysterical with fear whenever they see the police or soldiers near the house. Their mother is receiving treatment for severe psychological trauma. One family member told us:

It was as though they used the house for
target practice. It was so deliberate. We can
patch up the house, but I can never patch up
all the children who were shot.[80]

----

80. Interview by Helena Cook, Cape Town, November 15, 1985.

CHAPTER IV

Abuses by the SADF Against Children

In recent months there has been an increasing number of serious abuses against children by soldiers in the army units deployed in the townships to assist the police force. Most of these soldiers are young white conscripts. In the eyes of the residents, who feel themselves to be under military occupation, the mere presence of the army is a symbol of the government's determination to crush all opposition by the use of force. "Troops out of the townships" has been taken up as one of the rallying cries -- and non-negotiable demands -- of opposition groups.

During the State of Emergency soldiers were granted the same far-reaching powers as the police.[81] Although their role is essentially to support and assist police in the townships, soldiers have maintained a campaign of terror on their own initiative, and they frequently act without regard for the law. Their victims are generally taken to remote areas of scrubland or "veld" outside the townships or held inside armored vehicles, indicating that the soldiers are aware they are acting extra-judicially.

A. Short-Term Abductions

In the past year, a terrifying pattern of abuse has emerged in townships with a heavy military presence: soldiers pick up children on the streets, load them into casspirs (armored vehicles) and hold them for several nightmarish hours. Inside the casspirs, the children are threatened, intimidated and assaulted before being turned out to make their own way home.

Since these children are not formally arrested, such incidents do not appear in any statistics. It is, therefore, impossible to ascertain the extent of these abuses. However, from the affidavits it has collected, the Detainees' Parents

----

81. See Chapter II.F., supra.

Support Committee (DPSC) is convinced that abuses by the army are a serious and growing problem and probably far more widespread than anyone in the human rights community had realized.

Some of the children who have gone to DPSC to recount their experiences at the hands of soldiers have been visited by the army again, sometimes more than once. As a result, some children who are abused or threatened by the army are too scared to come forward and tell their story.

Seventeen year-old Siphiwe was at home in Soweto on October 9, 1985 when two soldiers suddenly came into the house. They dragged Siphiwe outside, slapped him in the face and forced him to run along the streets followed by the casspir:

> They told me not to speak to anyone as they would let me go and then shoot me. Later they put me in the casspir. They made me sit on the floor. There were about 8 soldiers in the casspir.
>
> One soldier . . . asked me to give the names and addresses of COSAS members.[82] I could not as I did not know any. They then put a perfume like stuff on my hands and made me rub my hands and inhale it. It made me dizzy. They poured it on my hair . . . [and one] held a cigarette near me.
>
> The casspir stopped at a circle in White City. A number of other casspirs also stopped and a soldier from one of the other casspirs came into our casspir. He started beating me with his fists and my mouth and nose were bleeding. A number of soldiers were kicking me back and forth between them. They then pulled my hair and someone else was stamping on my shoulders. As one of the soldiers hit me, I ducked and when he hurt

----

82. As previously noted, COSAS is a broad-based student organization, now banned.

his hand against the casspir, he made me lick the blood off his hand. I tried to hide behind one soldier but he took his rifle and hit me on my face with the rifle butt. Another stamped on my neck while I was lying on the floor of the casspir. One of the soldiers also poured water up my nose while another held my head back by my hair.[83]

Siphiwe overheard the soldiers discussing what they would do with him. They decided not to take him to the police station because they were afraid they might get into trouble as Siphiwe was bleeding and badly injured. Instead, they "threw me out of the casspir . . . while the casspir was still moving." Two men who found Siphiwe gave him a lift home.

Another 17 year-old boy was picked up in Diepkloof on October 23, 1985 by soldiers and was taken to a remote area in the veld beyond the township. They asked if he was a member of COSAS:

One beat me with his fists and bent my thumbs back. They made me sit on the ground with my legs stretched out in front of me and apart. One soldier sat on each leg and they bent my fingers. One pushed his two fingers into my throat . . . . They kicked me on my back with their boots.[84]

Eventually the soldiers abandoned the youth in the veld, and he managed to hitch a lift home. The next day he was taken to a doctor for treatment.

A group of soldiers in Dobsonville used tracker dogs to hunt three boys who were hiding in a house on December 2, 1985. Two of the boys, who had been visiting some friends, had earlier seen a group of boys running away from three casspirs. The two were afraid that the soldiers would think they had been part of this group, so they ran into a

----

83. Statement, Johannesburg, 1985.

84. Statement, Johannesburg, November 1985.

neighbor's house where the third boy, Arthur, was asleep in bed.

The soldiers pulled Arthur, who is 15, out by his hair and beat him severely with their fists and rifle butts. They sent in the dogs to find the other two boys, put all three into the casspir where they assaulted them. They then picked up two more boys, after forcing the first three to point out the homes of their friends. All were taken out to the veld. Eventually six casspir-loads of soldiers gathered there with the boys.

The soldiers set the dogs on the boys and kicked and sjambokked them, pouring petrol over one of them and holding a cigarette lighter near him. They tried to force the boys to tell them about the student organization COSAS, and the names of people who had thrown petrol bombs. When the boys could not give satisfactory replies, they were whipped and assaulted again. One of the boys overheard the soldiers saying that they should not go to the police station as they might be asked to explain the assaults. Fifteen year-old Arthur had been bitten and scratched by the dogs, and was so badly beaten that the soldiers eventually had to take him to the hospital for treatment. The soldiers then put him back in the casspir and eventually released him a long way from his home at about midnight.[85]

B. Short-Term Detentions at Army Barracks

The army has set up temporary barracks close to the townships for the soldiers stationed there. Some children have been abducted by soldiers and kept in these camps for several hours or even days. While detained at these camps, the children are often subjected to serious physical abuse.

One 12 year-old boy, Solomon, was taken from his bed at his home in Soweto on October 21, 1985 at 2:30 a.m. by five or six soldiers armed with rifles. The soldiers told Solomon's mother that they would take him to Orlando Police Station, but refused to tell her why. Inquiries by Solomon's family the next day at two different police stations were fruitless, and it seemed that Solomon had

----

85. Statements, Johannesburg, January 1985.

disappeared. The police suggested that his family contact the military base. The commander at the base admitted that children were being held there but still would not confirm Solomon's whereabouts. The family was told by a captain in the SADF that all the children being held at the base would be taken to a police station later that day.

In the evening the parents went back to the police station but were told their son was not there. At 11:30 that night the child suddenly appeared, having walked home after the soldiers left him about three kilometers away in a dangerous part of the township. At first, Solomon did not say much about his ordeal but complained the next day of a sore throat. He eventually told his mother that one of the soldiers had grabbed him by the throat and choked him until he could not breathe. He said he had been taken to the camp, beaten and forced to sleep outside on the ground without blankets or food.

The following day Solomon's mother went to the Detainees' Parents Support Group to recount what had happened. When she returned, Solomon was missing. She learned that the soldiers had returned in her absence and had taken the child away at gunpoint. Eventually she traced her son to Diepkloof prison. Her attorney telexed the Police Commissioner twice before the child was finally released after three days in prison.[86]

Joseph is a shy, quiet boy, only 14 years old. The fingernails of one of his hands are twisted and blackened, the result of electric shock treatment to which soldiers subjected him many times during the days he was kept, with some other children, at an army camp outside Daveyton. His wrist has a large burn mark where he was burned with a cigarette lighter. He was blindfolded when he was first picked up by the soldiers on September 19, 1985 while playing football, and does not know exactly where the camp is.[87]

----

86. Interview by Helena Cook, Johannesburg, November 28, 1985.

87. Interview by Helena Cook, Johannesburg, November 25, 1985.

For nine days, the soldiers terrorized Joseph and the other boys they had picked up with him. Joseph described how they were forced to get into a hole filled with sewage water up to their waists:

> We were told by one of the white soldiers that we should force each other's heads down beneath the water. . . . [At] times we were completely submerged beneath the water. I could not bear the filth that was in the water and consequently tried to climb out of the hole.

> One of the white soldiers who was standing next to the hole with a sjambok thrashed me a number of times. . . I started to scream . . . . [He] continued to thrash me so that I fell back into the filthy water.[88]

When Joseph persisted in trying to get out of the water, the soldiers took him into a van. When he sat down, they whipped him with a sjambok for making the seat dirty. They told him to identify some children in photographs they showed to him and, when he could not, they tortured him:

> Another white soldier took my right arm and bent it behind my back. He then took out a lighter . . . and he held it beneath the wrist of my right hand . . . the pain was excruciating and I could smell my flesh burning. I screamed and felt faint from the pain.[89]

The soldiers then tied a wire around Joseph's right hand that was attached to a box with "a handle like a telephone handle." According to Joseph:

> One of the soldiers turned the handle of this box a number of times and at the same time water was poured on my hand. I felt a

----

88. Affidavit, Johannesburg, December, 1985.

89. Id.

tremendous shock and great pain. . . . The soldiers continued to turn the handle of the green box and each time my body would convulse with the electric shocks and explode from the water. In exploding, it ripped out my thumbnail and took a chunk of flesh out of my thumb quite close to the first digit . . . . When the soldiers saw that my nail had been ripped out they took the wire from my thumb and tied it around my index finger just below the nail. They then turned the handle and poured water and shocked me a number of times. The pain was so intense that I almost fainted. I remember feeling dizzy and very nauseous.[90]

The soldiers repeated the electric shock treatment on two other fingers, leaving another ugly scar. On each of the next seven days at the camp Joseph was tortured again. "On these occasions I was given electric shock treatment and kicked and beaten repeatedly," he said. The soldiers cut Joseph's leg with a broken soft drink bottle, leaving a wound that later became infected.[91] Joseph and the other boys were given no food during most of their period in the camp, and the only water they drank came from the sewage hole. They slept outside on the ground without any cover. Joseph remembers that one of the white soldiers spoke Zulu and, when the others were not around, he tried to talk to the boys. He warned them not to try to run away because the other soldiers would shoot them dead.[92] On the ninth day three other boys were brought in. The new arrivals were taken into a van and tortured one by one. That night, Joseph and the rest were finally taken to the police station at Modderbee.

Following his harrowing experience in the camp, Joseph was detained in prison for a further 13 days. According to Joseph, a district surgeon who examined him

----

90. Id.

91. Interview by Dayle Powell, Johannesburg, November 1985.

92. Interview by Helena Cook, Johannesburg, November 25, 1985.

told him that his account of what the soldiers had done was a lie and that the injuries on his hands showed that he must have been carrying a petrol bomb. He was not given proper treatment in prison for his wounds, which became infected.

Since his release, Joseph has seen the soldiers who tortured him several times on patrol in the township. On two occasions, his house has again been visited by soldiers, apparently looking for him. He is now terrified of being arrested and tortured again.

CHAPTER V

Security Forces in the Schools

Black schools in the townships are the site of frequent, and often violent, confrontations between the security forces and school children. Schools have become primary targets in the attempts by police and the army to crush student organization and mobilization, which has increasingly been orchestrated at the schools as opportunities for holding legal gatherings elsewhere have been restricted.[93]

At first, protest actions in South African schools addressed grievances pertaining to the vastly inferior educational opportunities for blacks, particularly Africans. State education in South Africa is administered on a segregated basis. In 1984 only R234 were spent on the education of each African child, as compared to R1654 for each white child. African schooling is neither free nor compulsory.[94] The schools are poorly equipped and overcrowded, and the staff are inexperienced and under-qualified. Four-fifths of them have not even completed high school themselves. In 1984, the pupil-teacher ratio for Africans was 40:1, as compared with 19:1 for whites. As a result, only 25% of black secondary school pupils reach the final year, Standard 10. Of the small minority of African pupils who took the matriculation examination required for university entry in 1983, less than 50% of them passed, compared with 80% of white pupils.[95] For these reasons, schools have been the site of frequent protest actions, typically in the form of boycotts by the pupils. As one headmaster put it:

----

93. See Chapter II, supra.

94. Education in African schools is compulsory only where the school committees have specifically requested it. At present, compulsory schooling affects only 6.7% of African school children.

95. Race Relations Survey 1984, South African Institute of Race Relations, 1985.

The school is associated with everything [the
pupils] hate. It is a symbol of inferiority,
state control. . . . It is a symbol of everything
that makes their teenage years of very little
value, so it's a natural target for them.[96]

School boycotts, which occurred sporadically in 1983,
became increasingly widespread and prolonged in 1984 and
1985. The boycotts were initially organized in support of
educational demands, including compulsory, free education;
qualified teachers; appropriate textbooks; democratically
elected student representative councils; and an end to sexual
harassment of girl pupils by teachers and to corporal
punishment.

One of the first victims of the police response to the
latest wave of boycotts and student protest was 15 year-old
Emma Sathege. Emma was run over by a police van and
killed during confrontations in Atteridgeville, Pretoria when
students boycotted classes there in January 1984. As the
civil unrest intensified during the following months, the
school boycotts spread rapidly.

Student demands broadened beyond educational
grievances to incorporate the political issues that were giving
rise to increasing protests. These included the new
Constitution, the hated town councils, high rents and other
economic grievances. During the State of Emergency,
students took up the grievances engendered by the increased
repression. They called for the lifting of the State of
Emergency; the removal of military troops from the
townships; the release of all political detainees, especially
teachers and fellow pupils; and an end to the security forces'
onslaught against pupils on school premises.

In August 1985 the student organization COSAS was
banned. At the same time, orders issued pursuant to the
emergency regulations required pupils to be inside the

----

96. "School Boycott is Erasing Dreams in South Africa," New York Times,
December 1, 1985.

classrooms during school hours and forbade them to participate in unauthorized extra-curricular activities.[97]

A. Military Operations in the Schools

To enforce these restrictions, both police and army units intensified operations in the schools during the State of Emergency. Units of the South African Defense Force (SADF) frequently patrolled school premises in armored vehicles. There were numerous reports of the security forces entering the schools, arresting any pupils not in class, going into the classrooms, harrassing and arresting teachers and pupils, assaulting and sjambokking[98] children, throwing tear gas into school grounds and even inside classrooms, opening fire at random and generally maintaining a highly visible, provocative and intimidating presence.

These measures exacerbated an already tense situation, and increased the likelihood of violent confrontation. Pleas by teachers and school principals for the police and army to stay out of the schools were usually ignored. Indeed, the staff themselves became victims of the violence and brutality as well. Anyone who attempted to protect the children or defuse a likely confrontation was likely to be labelled a sympathizer or accused of encouraging student protests. Such teachers were arrested and detained, which further inflamed the situation.

On August 29, 1985, at a Cape Town school where some pupils had been involved in boycotts and protest rallies, police launched a full-scale attack on the school even though there was no trouble at the school on that day. A group of some 20 children were preparing to leave school and were fired at with rubber bullets by three plainclothes policemen. At this, many other children came out of the

----

97. Government Notice No. 1799, August 8, 1985. Subsequent notices were issued later in August and again in October extending the control of school boycotts to other areas governed by the State of Emergency.

98. As noted earlier, a sjambok is a hide whip with a sharp metal tip.

classrooms to see what was happening. According to the principal's report:

> Within fifteen minutes, virtually the whole police force, or so it appeared, had cordoned off the school grounds, and viciously bombarded us with teargas and rubber bullets.[99]

The tear gas was so dense that "only the roof of the building was visible at one stage," and teachers and pupils sought refuge inside the school:

> When the police realized that they had us trapped like animals inside the buildings, they moved onto the grounds, smashed our windows, threw gas bombs inside the classrooms, wood work rooms and administration block . . . . Conditions inside [these areas] were like the gas chambers of Auschwitz.[100]

The principal attempted to appeal to one policeman, but "instead of giving me a hearing he attacked me with his sjambok, narrowly missing me and smashed the glass door." After numerous calls to police headquarters, the police captain finally ordered his men to withdraw. The school gates were unlocked and parents and neighbours were brought into the school to help carry outside all the children overcome by tear gas fumes.

Similar incidents took place in numerous schools during the State of Emergency. At Vista High School in Cape Town on September 3, 1985, for example, police stormed into the school and arrested several pupils after debris had been set alight outside the premises. Police fired shots over the heads of teachers on the school grounds, and

----

99. Report of the Principal to the Regional Director of the Department of Education and Culture, September 3, 1985.

100. Id.

two policemen burst into the school and pointed a gun at 20 teachers and pupils, saying, "I will just shoot you dead."[101]

Police action has by no means been confined to areas governed by the Emergency. On September 6, 1985, for example, police launched an apparently unprovoked attack on Lamontville High School in Durban, seriously wounding 12 children, many of whom required hospitalization. The incident began at 9:00 a.m., when police arrived and threw tear gas at the school. They entered the school premises, sjambokked the pupils as they tried to flee, and shot at some of them. "I am doing it for law and order," a policeman told Mr. P., a member of staff. "If you cannot take care of the children, we will do the job for you."[102]

Mr. P., who first realized what was happening when he heard "screams coming from all around the school premises," attempted to protect the children. He said, "I held one [policeman] by the collar of his jacket who was beating [a child] who was lying on the ground and bleeding from a large wound in his head."[103]

Some of the children tried to hide and were pursued by police and whipped when they were caught. Phillip, aged 14, was in the school kitchen:

> Many policemen suddenly came into the kitchen. They were all dressed in blue . . . and carrying sjamboks. They began hitting me and all the other children who were in the kitchen . . . .
>
> I tried to run away, but they followed me to the staff room . . . . One began hitting me with a sjambok on my legs. I was so badly hurt that when the policeman stopped hitting

---

101. "Police raid Bo-Kaap school, arrest pupils," Cape Times, September 3, 1985.

102. Affidavit, Durban, September 1985.

103. Id.

me I crawled to the staffroom and hid there.[104]

Other children were injured when they jumped from second floor classrooms to escape the police. One of these children described how he was beaten until he managed to barricade himself in a classroom:

> The police came inside with whips and sjamboks . . . . I got into the classroom and jumped from a window two stories to the ground. I hurt my ankle badly. When I got up from the ground, a lot of police were around, one started hitting me with a sjambok. I tried to escape . . . and another policeman hit me with a whip. I was hit on the arm and thigh. I managed to get into the classroom where I barricaded myself in with desks across the door.[105]

Police also shot at children to stop them from running away. The boy that Mr. P. had attempted to protect described what he remembered before he lost consciousness:

> Some teargas had been thrown in the school grounds. I could smell it and see the smoke . . . . I saw the police chasing pupils in the school grounds. I then jumped out of the window because I felt I would be cornered if I remained in the classroom . . . . One of the policeman shouted that if I went on running away he would shoot me. Suddenly I felt a bang on my head. I can't remember what happened after that as I lost consciousness . . . . [At the hospital] I had seven stitches put into the right side of my head.[106]

----

104. Affidavit, Durban, September 1985.

105. Affidavit, Durban, September 1985.

106. Affidavit, Durban, September 1985.

Two pupils received stitches for head and facial injuries and others required first aid treatment after police entered the Fred Guam secondary school in Ceres in late October 1985, and beat pupils with sjamboks. This was apparently in response to the stoning of a police van in the township some days earlier. The police hit pupils at random, lashing them across their faces, arms and shoulders. A police spokesman in Pretoria defended the action saying that those who instigated violence should take cognizance of the possible result of their lawless behavior.[107]

Interviews with teachers from various schools in the townships outside Cape Town reveal a pervasive pattern of terrorization of South Africa's schools by security forces during the State of Emergency:

> Police control the schools and they walk in at any time to check that a teacher is teaching the prepared classes. If a child is not in school by 8:00 a.m. he or she is immediately arrested. The police assault children whenever they catch them. Girls often get caught because they do not run as fast. They are frequently beaten across the face and breasts.

* * * *

> By mid-August [1985] police were always coming into the schools and would shoot at random. Casspirs stood outside on the road with a soldier reading out the boycott regulations through a megaphone.

* * * *

> I was present when the police tried to break up one march and blocked the route with casspirs. Eight riot police came marching down the road towards the children carrying shotguns and whips. Half the children ran into a bog at the side of the road and many

---

107. "Ceres Pupils 'beaten'," Cape Times, October 31, 1985.

collapsed into the water from the effects of the teargas. Others tried to run and were caught and viciously beaten.

* * * *

Last Friday at school the casspirs arrived. A boy in Standard 6, only 13 years old, was arrested and charged with intimidation. They beat him across the face while they questioned him.

* * * *

I saw one riot policeman shooting at two small children who were running away; he was aiming directly at them.

* * * *

The riot police and soldiers come and go from our schools constantly. They terrorize the children and have threatened some of them with detention, torture and even sodomy. Some of the kids are scared to death, others are angry. The atmosphere is so tense and the teachers are caught in the middle. It is impossible to carry on classes under these conditions.[108]

The police were particularly determined to prevent any kind of activity at schools that did not constitute class teaching of the approved curriculum. They would move in immediately to break up meetings or suspected gatherings, regardless of their purpose.

At a Port Elizabeth secondary school two children were killed when police attempted to break up a meeting between staff and student representatives on July 24, 1985. According to a teacher at the school, Mr. S., the meeting was already adjourned when police arrived and scaled the school fence, threatening that they would control the

----

108. Interviews by Helena Cook, Cape Town, November 19, 1985.

children if the teachers could not. An argument ensued and the police started "firing wildly." Many children panicked and some tried to escape over the fence. Two of these children were killed. Mr. S. persuaded others to stay in the classrooms in order to avoid more casualties. He now fears that he has been singled out by the police as a sympathizer with the children and that, as a result, both his job and his life may be in jeopardy.[109]

Peaceful rallies organized by students and any meetings at which political issues might be discussed were swiftly broken up by the security forces. In early September 1985, Cape Town students organized a peaceful march in the middle of the city, in part to alert some of the white residents to their grievances. For many white people, shielded from the unrest in the isolated townships, it was their first sight of the routine brutality of the police toward children. One shocked white man said the students were "singing softly" when police suddenly arrived to "lay into them" with whips. The witness heard no warning from the police that the children should disperse. He said:

> The kids just scattered in all directions, most were severely beaten. Several of the kids were bundled into police vans and driven away.[110]

On another occasion in July 1985, police again lit into a group of school children with whips as the children were attempting to board buses to attend a mass rally at the University of the Western Cape. The school principal had gone out to express his disagreement with their decision and to warn them of the dangers of attending an illegal rally. He stated that they were "very orderly" and "listened to me very attentively and quietly."[111] No police were present. Minutes after the principal left, he heard the pupils running and saw that "a contingent of about 30 policemen had

----

109. Statement, Port Elizabeth, July 31, 1985.

110. "Police Whips Silence Protest," Cape Times, September 5, 1985.

111. Report of the Principal to the Regional Director of Administration, July 29, 1985.

arrived and sjambokked the children," despite the fact that "the children had responded almost IMMEDIATELY to the instruction for them to leave the two buses." When the principal objected, the captain in charge threatened him with the loss of his job. Eighty-seven of the children "had welts on their faces, legs and other parts of their bodies," and one girl required hospital treatment.

Another teacher described to the Lawyers Committee a meeting he attended at Wynberg Secondary School in Cape Town at which a United Democratic Front executive member, Graeme Bloc, had been asked to speak to the children. About 2000 pupils, aged 6-18 years, and a number of teachers were present:

> Three police gave the principal 30 minutes to stop the meeting, which they said was a "political rally." The headmaster attempted to do so but the children would not disperse. In the end Graeme got up and managed to speak for about 10 minutes until one policeman lost patience, rushed onto the platform and seized the microphone. He pinned Graeme's arms behind him and marched him off the stage. Two other police drew their guns on the children, who were both angry and very frightened by this time. I was terrified that the young children would panic and the police would start shooting . . . . Police outside the hall gave us three minutes to clear out before they came in.
>
> As I left the school premises with three young pupils the casspirs were circling around. A tyre was burning nearby and a police van drew up beside us. The police roughly questioned the pupils with me and threatened to detain them if they were ever caught near another fire.[112]

The conduct of the security forces in the schools substantially contributed to the volatile situation, although

----

112. Interview by Helena Cook, Cape Town, November 11, 1985.

the police were always careful to report that they were merely responding to disruption and violence started by pupils. For example, after the Wynberg meeting was forced to disperse, a few of the pupils were so angry and frustrated by the police behavior that they walked out of school, went into the town and damaged several cars and shop windows. The SABC news report, taken from the official police account, stated that the police had moved into Wynberg School only *after* pupils had damaged property.

Even young children were put at risk. In Soweto, during disturbances at an adjacent high school on August 25, 1985, police fired tear gas into the Entokozweni Early Learning Center in Soweto, where there were more than 100 infants aged six months to two years old. Many were knocked unconscious by the fumes, and others vomited. When the principal sought emergency assistance from the police for the badly affected children, the police merely told her to contact a hospital.[113]

Two days earlier, again in Soweto, police arrested 300 students, some as young as seven years old. The *Star* newspaper asked Police Commissioner Brigadier Coetzee to comment on the fact that some of these children were only seven years old and quoted him as saying that this was "quite possible." Later the Brigadier denied having said this to the press.

B. Mass Arrests at Schools

Two examples of the random and indiscriminate nature of arrests and detention of school children occurred in Soweto shortly after the declaration of the State of Emergency, when hundreds of school children were arrested en masse, creating chaos and confusion at the local police station.

----

113. Democratic Movement Under Attack - A Report on the State of Emergency July-September 1985, DPSC and DESCOM, October 1985, at 29.

An attorney who represented some of these children told the Lawyers Committee that, on August 22, 1985, 320 schoolchildren were arrested by the SADF and brought to Moroka Police Station. All of them were held in police cells overnight. The following day, when the attorneys arrived, the police said that they were prepared to release all the children without charge. The public prosecutor of the local magistrates court insisted, however, that they must be charged before they could be released. As a result, 291 children were charged with contravention of an emergency regulation, and all were then released into their parents' custody.

The regulation required children to be within school premises during specified hours. Yet a number of the children said they had been arrested inside the school grounds or outside at legitimate break-times or on their way home after school had been dismissed. All of those charged were required to appear in court on the following Monday. When half the children did not appear, no warrants for their arrest were issued and the charges against them apparently lapsed. The case against the remainder who were in court was remanded until October 15, 1985. On that day, all remaining charges were simply withdrawn.[114]

The attorney also told the Lawyers Committee that while she was at the police station to negotiate the release of these children from custody on August 23, 1985,

> [t]ruckloads of other children began arriving. There must have been about 600 of them and some were very young. It was pandemonium. The police would not let the parents through the gates so the parents were angry and many of the children were screaming and very upset.[115]

The new arrivals who were under 13 years old were separated from the others. Parents began to arrive but were forbidden by police to enter the station yard. Officials

----

114. Interview by Helena Cook, Johannesburg, November 21, 1985.

115. Id.

could not process all the children, which exacerbated the already tense situation. After negotiations with the District Commissioner of Police, Brigadier Coetzee, and with the intervention of Bishop Desmond Tutu, all these children were eventually released without charge. A police officer told one of the lawyers that it had been absurd for the SADF to arrest more people than they could process.[116]

Several weeks later, all 786 pupils and their teachers at a school in Soweto were arrested. According to a teacher at the school, a few of the children had been boycotting classes, although they were present at the school. As a result, there was a heavy army and police presence around the school all week, and the principal was warned that all pupils must attend classes. On September 12, 1985, the teacher noticed "an unusually large number of casspirs" at the school and "numerous soldiers started to file . . . into the school yard." The teachers and principal pleaded with the officer in charge, Major Kotze, to let them handle the situation as the presence of the security forces would only make matters worse. Major Kotze responded: "We are going to arrest all the children in the school." Then,

> [a] black policemen shouted through a loud hailer . . . that everybody in the school is under arrest . . . . Many of [the children] burst into tears. Most of the children appeared to be consumed with fear and distress . . . .[117]

The children were ordered into waiting trucks. The teacher noted that "the police and soldiers were heavily armed," and he attempted to supervise the children to keep the situation calm. He said:

> A soldier pulled me aside and told me to go away. As I walked away . . . the soldier turned around and punched me on the nose . . . . Children were being loaded into the

----

116. Memorandum prepared by Lawyers for Human Rights (undated).

117. Founding affidavit of Lunga Mboba, Lunga Mboba and others v. The Divisional Commissioner of Police: Soweto, September 14, 1985.

trucks as they entered and removed from the
school premises. When the last three trucks
were to be loaded, police went to the
classrooms to look for any children who
might still be there. These children were
ordered by the police to leave the classrooms
and to go to the trucks. Some of them were
even carried out of the classrooms by
policemen and soldiers.[118]

The children and teachers were taken to the police
station. A mother who had witnessed the arrests tried to
take warm clothing to her two daughters but police refused
to accept it. When lawyers arrived they were told the
arrests had been made because "the school had been
troublesome for the whole of this week." According to one
attorney present, Major Kotze also said:

> The children have not been charged. They
> have been detained in terms of the emergency
> regulations. I am entitled to hold them for
> fourteen days and the order can be
> renewed.[119]

He later agreed to release all children under 12 years old.
An attorney told the Lawyers Committee:

> The atmosphere at the police station was very
> tense. Parents and teachers were very angry
> and the children were lining the passage
> ways. Some of them were crying. The police
> were very unhelpful and aggressive to the
> lawyers and told us we were in the way and
> why were we here. We went to see the
> Divisional Commissioner who told us the
> children have been told to "keep the country
> ungovernable". He would not release any of
> them.[120]

----

118. Id.

119. Affidavit of Fiona Grace McLachlan.

120. Interview by Helena Cook, Johannesburg, November 21, 1985.

The children were kept in police cells overnight and early the next day an urgent application was brought in the Supreme Court for their release. Before the application was heard, the police agreed to release all the children, who were freed at 6:15 p.m. that day.

C. Examination-Period Violence

The situation in the schools reached its worst point in mid-November 1985, as end-of-year examinations were due to take place. Some teachers and many pupils called for the examinations to be postponed because, after so much disruption, even the pupils who wished to write were woefully unprepared to do so. The examinations went ahead under extremely tense and intimidating circumstances.

Some of those who wanted to write were taken to military bases to do so. Other pupils who went to school tore up their examination papers as a gesture of defiance, while others pretended to write but filled the pages with drawings, slogans or other trivia. The police and the army moved in, brandishing weapons, to patrol the classrooms and to "protect" those who wished to sit for the examinations. Anyone in class who was not writing risked assault and arrest, as did teachers who refused to invigilate under such conditions. A teacher told reporters:

> The police behavior is bizarre. They go through the classrooms, check the scripts, not knowing what they are doing. Imagine writing an exam with a huge cop carrying a shotgun leaning over your shoulder checking what you are writing, especially when a week or two back those same cops were firing birdshot and tear gas at you and sometimes killing your buddies.[121]

Another remarked:

----

121. "The new language of township education," Cape Times, November 23, 1985.

The exams are taking place under the most abnormal conditions one could find anywhere. Teachers and students are in detention, harassment of teachers and students continues without any break, there is no concern for the educational interests of the students, it is rather a matter of the authority of the State being forced onto the students. These exams are not a part of an educational process, but part of a political power game.[122]

At Kasselsvlei Senior Secondary School in Cape Town, a group of 44 children aged about 14 tore up their exam papers and were all arrested, together with four teachers. Police also fired several rounds of tear gas, according to one teacher, and later returned to arrest the deputy principal, a department head and another teacher. The girls and a female teacher were subsequently released, but the boys remained in custody.[123]

Another teacher told the Lawyers Committee:

Last Tuesday exams started. Promptly at 8:15 a.m. a "sneeze machine"[124] and police vehicles arrived and they detained a teacher. Two army casspirs drove into the school. Of course the students became very angry and large numbers of them left the school.

The casspirs were later withdrawn. Instead, ten police walked in with shotguns. They patrolled up and down the aisles in the classrooms checking what the students were writing.[125]

----

122. Id.

123. "Arrests after pupils tear exams papers," Argus, November 15, 1985.

124. This refers to a police vehicle used to fire cannisters of tear gas.

125. Interview by Helena Cook, Cape Town, November 19, 1985.

- 74 -

The nationwide agreement by most pupils to return to school in January 1986 has not restored peace to the schools. On the day before the return, a 15 year-old school girl, Franscina Legoete, was killed in clashes with the police in Kagiso township near Krugersdorp. According to a school chaplain, the pupils were holding an orderly and lawful meeting to discuss whether they should return to school, when police started firing tear gas and rubber bullets. Some pupils were injured as they tried to escape and 13 had to be taken to the hospital. Franscina died on arrival.[126]   Police in Lansdowne went into a secondary school and marched from class to class, interrogating the staff and ordering them to teach, although only 8% of the pupils were in school. The Western Cape Teachers Union condemned "this unwarranted and provocative action of police."[127]

The lifting of the State of Emergency has not curbed the violence of the security forces either. Children at school remain at risk and boycotts are immediately responded to with typical brutality.

----

126. "2 die in clashes with police," Cape Times, January 29, 1986.

127. "Police action at school criticized," Cape Times, January 25, 1986.

CHAPTER VI

Arrests of Children

Arrest and detention have been employed on a massive scale by security forces seeking to suppress protest activity, and thousands of children have fallen within the sweep of these practices. Some have been as young as seven years old.

Police frequently use intimidating tactics when making arrests. These include using large numbers of police (up to 20 have been reported in some cases), often in plainclothes and unmarked cars. Arrests frequently are made late at night or in the early hours of the morning. Lights are shone in the occupants' faces so that the arresting officers cannot be identified. Children are taken from their beds without an opportunity to dress properly or to take warm clothing with them.

On occasion, when the person wanted is not at home, the security forces have taken family members, including young children, into custody in an attempt to force the intended arrestee to go to the police station. When police came to arrest one woman in Letaba on September 18, 1985, and did not find her at home, they ordered her three children, aged 12, ten and five years, into the police van. They later released the younger two but took the 12 year-old girl into custody. She finally was released when her older sister went and pleaded with police to let the child go.[128]

At the time of arrest, children and their parents frequently are not informed of the reason for arrest. This makes it a difficult and lengthy process to ascertain whether there are grounds for challenging the arrest and what rights, if any, the child can assert, such as the right to see a lawyer or to be visited while in prison. Most children have little idea what rights they possess and, in any event, are usually

----

128. Statement, Johannesburg, November 24, 1985.

too frightened by the experience to attempt to enforce their rights.

These children are extremely vulnerable. Past practice has shown that those arrested under legal provisions that permit lengthy detention without charge and give the police virtually unfettered discretion in their treatment of such detainees face a particularly high risk of abuse by police.

During the unrest, children generally have been arrested pursuant to one of three laws: the Internal Security Act, the Criminal Procedure Act and, during the period of the State of Emergency, the emergency regulations. Some of these children have been released without charge after several hours or a few days in custody. Many of those arrested under the emergency regulations were detained without charge for 14 days, the maximum period that, according to the regulations, could be authorized by an ordinary police officer without an order of the Minister of Law and Order. Other children have been detained for periods of several months or more, indicating that an authority higher than the arresting officer explicitly sanctioned the child's continued incarceration.

A. Arrest Under the Internal Security Act

Children are among those arrested and detained under various provisions of the state's security legislation -- the Internal Security Act (ISA).[129] During 1985, more than 3600 people were arrested under the ISA, over three times the number of security arrests made during the previous year. Under the ISA persons can be arrested if they are suspected of committing offenses against the state such as terrorism, subversion and sabotage, or if they are otherwise believed to be endangering the security of the state or the maintenance of law and order. The Act also provides for such persons to be detained indefinitely without charge in order to prevent such offenses from being committed (Section 28) or for the purpose of interrogation (Section 29).

----

129. Act No. 74 of 1982. For discussion of this law, see Chapter II.D., supra.

Judicial review of arrest and detention pursuant to these provisions is effectively ousted. If the Minister of Law and Order or the appropriate police officer has properly ordered such detention within the terms of the very broad discretion set forth in the Act, no court has the power to pronounce upon the validity of the detention.

The detention provisions of the ISA expressly override all other statutory or common law provisions. Thus, for example, special provisions relating to the care and protection of juveniles in the Child Care Act,[130] the Prisons Act[131] or in any other legislation are of no effect when children are detained pursuant to the ISA.

The ISA authorizes *incommunicado* detention, a particularly harsh experience for children in any case, and one that also increases the risk of police abuse. Since detention without trial was first enacted into law in the 1960s, numerous allegations have been made concerning the torture and abuse of security detainees. The experience of Eugene Dlamini, a 16 year-old youth, is typical. Eugene was arrested in Durban on August 27, 1985 and detained under Section 29 of the ISA. He was so badly assaulted by the police that he required hospitalization and surgery after only five days in detention (see Chapter VII, *infra*). A recent study in Cape Town[132] found that 83% of the 176 former security detainees interviewed claimed to have suffered some form of physical abuse while in detention, ranging from electric shocks, severe beating, strangulation, deprivation of food, water and sleep as well as a variety of forms of psychological torture.

Unlike emergency detainees, Section 29 detainees have a right to make "written representations" concerning their detention to a board of review to which the police must periodically furnish reasons for the continued detention. It is unlikely, however, that children would be able to make an adequate representation about their cases

----

130. Act No. 74 of 1983.

131. Act No. 8 of 1959.

132. A Study of Detention and Torture in South Africa -- Preliminary Report, Don Foster and Diane Sandler, September 1985.

even if they were aware of this right. Unlike Section 28 detainees, those detained under Section 29 are not permitted access to a legal representative to assist them in this regard. Section 29 detainees are also supposed to be visited regularly by a magistrate, a district surgeon and an Inspector of Detainees, but these provisions, which are not always observed, have proved inadequate to protect detainees from abuse.[133]

In response to a letter from the Committee of Concern for Children expressing grave concern about children detained under the ISA, the Minister of Law and Order stated, "should it at any time be necessary to detain a juvenile under [Section 29], special precautions will be taken to ensure the well-being of such person."[134] There is no indication, however, that any special precautions were taken in recent instances of children detained under Section 29. On the contrary, they have suffered the worst aspects of such detentions -- they have been held in solitary confinement, interrogated, denied access to family members or a lawyer, and some have been tortured.

At the end of November 1985, some former detainees from Diepkloof Prison in Johannesburg reported that they had seen two girls aged 14 and 16 who had been held in solitary confinement for more than two months, apparently under Section 29 of the ISA. In response to inquiries, police would confirm only that 16 year-old Monica Thabethe was being detained under Section 29, following her arrest on September 19, 1985. They would not, however, confirm the detention of Joan Gqeba, aged 14. When Joan was released, it was finally established that she had been arrested with Monica and detained under Section 29 of the ISA. Both girls were eventually released on December 5, 1986, after spending 77 days in solitary confinement. Although Section 29 provides for detention specifically for the purpose of interrogation, both girls stated that they had been questioned only during the first few days of their detention.

----

133. See Chapter VII.D., infra.

134. Letter from the Minister of Law and Order to the Chairman of the Committee of Concern for Children, 1985.

Children also are among those arrested under Section 50 of the ISA. This section provides for the arrest of anyone whose actions, in the opinion of the arresting officer, contribute to a state of public disturbance, disorder or riot. The person arrested can be held for 48 hours and detained thereafter, on the issuance of a magistrate's warrant, for a further 14 days.

Section 50 has been widely used throughout the unrest. According to recent government statistics, there were 1194 arrests made under Section 50 in 1985, compared to only 166 in 1984[135]. Since only 114 of those arrested in 1985 were charged and only eight of them convicted, it is clear that Section 50 is being used as a form of detention.

During the State of Emergency, Section 50 was widely used by police as an alternative to emergency detention in areas not subject to the emergency regulations. Immediately before the State of Emergency was declared in Cape Town on October 26, 1985, for example, police used Section 50 to arrest large numbers of people in sweeps throughout the townships. As soon as the Emergency was declared there, those arrests and detentions were "converted" to emergency detentions, thus bypassing the need to obtain a magistrate's warrant for further detention.

Since the State of Emergency was lifted, there has been a sharp increase in Section 50 arrests. In Aliwal North during the last week of March 1986, at least 35 children, some only 11 years old, were arrested and detained under Section 50. A representative of the Youth Congress in the township has stated that he believes the arrests were made to prevent the children from attending the funeral of a 19 year-old woman who was shot dead by police during a consumer boycott. Residents reported that police were "roaming" the streets picking up the children. Several of the detainees are only 11 and 12 years old, while the others are aged between 13 and 17 years. The Youth Congress fears that as many as 70 children may have been arrested, but attorneys so far have the names of only 35. When residents

----

135. "Apartheid Barometer," Weekly Mail, April 4-10, 1986.

called a work "stayaway" to protest the arrests, the water supply to the township was deliberately cut off.[136]

Zelda Newman is a 15 year-old school girl who was arrested in Cape Town under Section 50 of the ISA on October 16, 1985 and detained for 14 days. Some of the pupils at Zelda's school had been boycotting classes. On October 9, 1985, the children organized a peaceful march to a nearby school timed to coincide with a "Day of Prayer" in the community. Police broke up the march, sjambokked[137] and beat the children, and told them to "run for their lives."

Zelda was arrested shortly after this. Within hours of her arrest, a magistrate issued a warrant authorizing her detention for 14 days for contributing to a state of public disturbance and disorder. She apparently was singled out for arrest because she was a member of the Student Representative Council (SRC) at her school. Three of the other five girls on the SRC also were arrested and detained under Section 50. In court proceedings challenging the validity of her detention, Zelda stated that she was a devout Christian committed to non-violence, and that neither she nor the SRC had advocated or organized the boycotts. The SRC had organized the march, but it was peaceful at all times until the police moved in with sjamboks to break it up. In any event, the warrant was issued before Zelda was questioned about her involvement by police. She was not permitted to say anything in her defense in front of the magistrate.[138]

B. Arrest Under the Criminal Procedure Act

The current unrest, which at times has involved outbreaks of stone throwing, rioting and damage to property, has given rise to an enormous increase in arrests

----

136. "35 children detained in 'no-water' Karoo town," Weekly Mail, March 21-27, 1986.

137. As previously noted, a sjambok is a metal-tipped whip.

138. Zelda Lorna Newman and John Charles Newman v. The Minister of Law and Order and three others, Cape Provincial Division, October 24, 1985.

pursuant to the Criminal Procedure Act.[139] The majority of
those arrested for criminal offenses have been charged with
public violence, a vaguely defined common law crime.
Detainees' Parents Support Committee (DPSC) estimates that,
in 1985, as many as 25,000 people were arrested and charged
with public violence and related offenses, such as arson,
malicious damage to property and intimidation. Young
people, many under 14 years of age and therefore below the
age of full criminal responsibility,[140] have been particularly
targeted for arrest and prosecution for public violence.[141]

Public violence is a common law offense and courts
in South Africa have grappled with its definition for
decades. Its essential elements are a group of people acting
together to commit unlawful and intentional acts that are of
sufficient gravity to disturb the peace or endanger security
or the rights of others. As long ago as 1938, a Supreme
Court judge spoke of "the vagueness of this offense and . . .
the difficulty, if not impossibility, of giving it an exact
definition."[142] Public violence may overlap with assault,
arson, robbery, damage to property and other crimes, but
these crimes committed by an individual acting alone do not
constitute public violence.

1. Arbitrary Arrests

Accounts of numerous people charged with public
violence suggest that criminal arrests have been widespread
and arbitrary and often are based on highly questionable
evidence; many of those arrested were not involved in the
criminal activity for which they were charged. This is not

----

139. Act No. 51 of 1977.

140. Under South African common law children aged seven to 14 years are
presumed not to be responsible for criminal offenses unless and until the
presumption is rebutted. Children under the age of seven are deemed to
be "doli incapax" and have no criminal responsibility.

141. Review of 1985, Detainees' Parents Support Committee, January 31,
1986. There have been so many of these prosecutions that it has been
impossible systematically to record and monitor the arrests and trials for
public violence.

142. R. v. Salie, 1938 T.P.D. 136 at 137-8.

to deny that there has been a surge of criminal activity in the townships during the unrest. The rising tide of black anger has at times found expression in rioting and stone-throwing. Property has been damaged, and children have sometimes been involved in such incidents. Yet the security forces' net has been cast so widely and indiscriminately that it is clear that they are using the vaguely-defined offense of public violence as a convenient means to control, intimidate and incarcerate anyone involved in political protest, particularly students. Arrested under the criminal legislation, dealt with as ordinary criminals and therefore missing from the statistics of "political prisoners," these are the hidden victims of the current political upheavals.

Two aspects of these arrests are particularly disturbing. First, it appears that the charge of public violence is now being used against anyone suspected of such acts as throwing a stone and damaging property, without due regard to the essential elements of the offense that the conduct must involve a group activity of sufficient gravity to endanger public security. In practice, the prosecution has been able to establish these elements of the offense simply by referring to the ongoing civil unrest in the country, regardless of the situation in the particular township at the time the alleged offense took place.

Second, according to township residents, it is common for the security forces to conduct a sweep of the area where an incident has occurred, arresting anyone they encounter, regardless of the individual's involvement in the incident. Anyone running away, as children almost invariably do now when they see police or SADF vehicles, is particularly likely to be pursued and arrested.

James, aged 17, was simply walking home from a friend's house on September 4, 1985:

> When we came into Josephs Avenue we saw the casspirs chasing people, we walked on. The casspirs were between myself and my residence. I could not get to my residence because the police were firing tear gas and rubber bullets. I ran in the opposite direction of my residence because of fear that the police will hit me. A casspir chased me . . . .

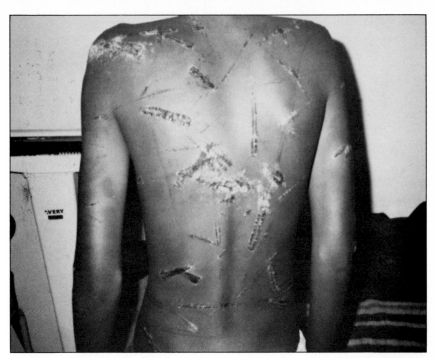

Young boy displays sjambok wounds sustained during a police attack in Mamelodi.

South African security forces with whips mount guard at a school in Soweto.
(Wendy Schwegman, courtesy of AFP photo.)

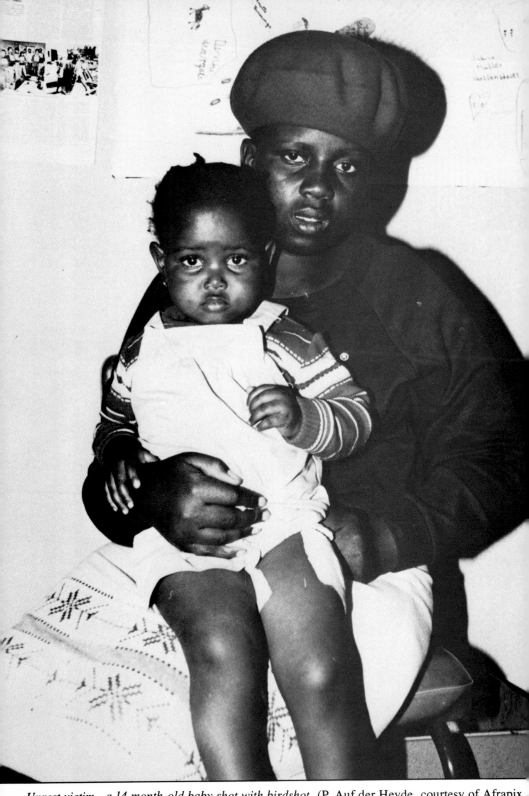

Unrest victim—a 14-month-old baby shot with birdshot. (P. Auf der Heyde, courtesy of Afrapix.

Security forces patrol a township outside Grahamstown after a funeral at which a child was killed when police opened fire on mourners. (Julian Covving, courtesy of Afrapix.)

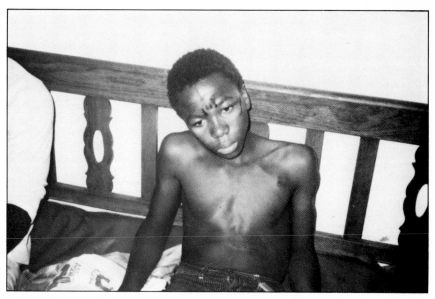

Child injured by the security forces in Mamelodi.

A 16-year-old youth lies dying after being shot by police at the funeral of eight unrest victims in New Brighton. (Steve Milton-Barber, courtesy of Afrapix.)

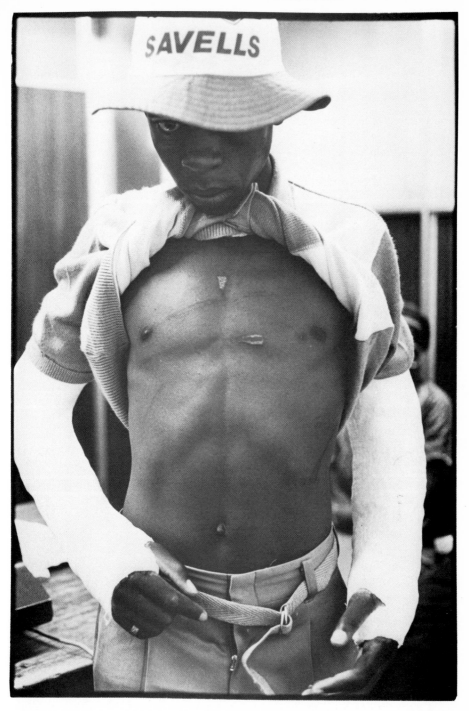

A 15-year-old boy displays injuries sustained while in detention. (Gill de Vlieg, courtesy of Afrapix.)

Eleven-year-old Fanie Goduka was arrested for public violence and held for 57 days in a prison cell with adult criminals (p. 89). (Helena Cook.)

These children, aged 11 and 13 years, were beaten and sjambokked by police when arrested during a night vigil for an unrest victim. (Gill de Vlieg, courtesy of Afrapix.)

Woman whose son was killed by police in Soweto. (Gill de Vlieg, courtesy of Afrapix.)

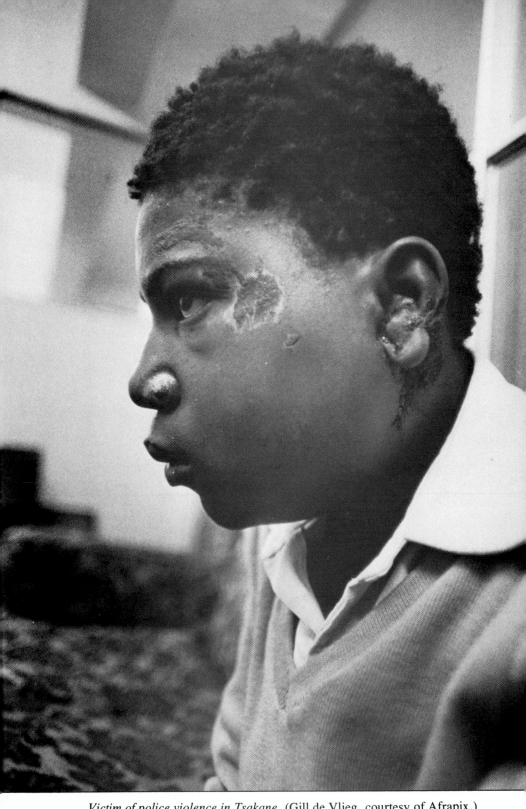

Victim of police violence in Tsakane. (Gill de Vlieg, courtesy of Afrapix.)

> The police from the casspir arrived and
> pointed the guns on me and ordered me to
> the casspir. I walked towards them, then
> they hit me with the sjamboks.[143]

At the police station, a constable threatened James "that he
is going to handcuff me to a bench until I revealed that I
was one of the stone throwers." James was beaten with a
baton, locked up for two days and charged with public
violence.

Emily, also 17, was coming home from a rugby
match on September 4, 1985. She saw people running away
from a casspir and heard shots. A man in front of her was
shot and she stopped to assist him. As she proceeded to go
home, she also was shot in the shoulder. She started to run
and took refuge in a nearby house, but "the police entered
and took me from the house. They put me in the casspir
and told me to lie down -- two of the policemen jumped on
my legs." At the police station she was sent to the hospital
for treatment, then brought back to the police station at 2
a.m., locked in a cell and charged with public violence.[144]

In October 1985 two 11 year-old boys were arrested
in Capetown on a charge of public violence. The police had
found one of them with an empty petrol can and alleged
that he had been making petrol bombs. The child is a fruit
vendor and uses the empty cans to support a makeshift stall.
He was beaten up, taken to the police station and held there
for four days until the first court hearing. The other child
was charged when police found him playing with a toy
catapult. Eventually, charges were withdrawn against both
boys.[145]

Ninety-four people were arrested on February 22,
1986 when police stormed into a night vigil for a victim
killed by the police in Mamelodi. All 94 were charged with
public violence and were denied bail until they obtained

----

143. Affidavit, Cape Town, September 19, 1985.

144. Affidavit, Cape Town, September 19, 1985.

145. Interview by Helena Cook, Cape Town, November 19, 1985.

legal representation after 17 days in jail. Of the 94, 80 were minors, and included a ten and 11 year-old, four 12 year-olds, and eight 13 year-old children.[146] One of those arrested was a sixteen year-old girl, who was detained for 17 days with her three month-old baby.

As noted in Chapter III.C., *supra*, anyone found by police to have birdshot or buckshot wounds risks a charge of public violence, regardless of how the injury was sustained. A mother in Kwa-Nobuhle township described how police burst into the doctor's office while she was waiting for an ambulance to take her unconscious 17 year-old son, Thembane, to the hospital. Thembane had been shot by police as he left his house to go to the store. The police asked who had been shot and directed the nurses to carry the boy to a waiting van. They also took an eight year-old boy who had shot wounds and was very distressed, as well as a 12 year-old girl who was unconscious. Thembane apparently regained consciousness; his mother could hear him screaming as the van drove away. The police appeared to have no equipment in the van to deal with injured people. Thembane told his mother later that the police had placed their spare wheel on top of him in the van.[147] X-rays revealed that birdshot had lodged above both of Thembane's eyes, in his thighs, arms, neck and chest, requiring surgery. The police subsequently charged him with public violence.

2. The Right to Counsel

Children arrested for public violence have the right to see a lawyer, but many do not know this and there is no duty imposed on the police or the magistrate to inform them. Obtaining legal representation is made more difficult still by the fact that parents generally are not told when their child will appear in court. In any event, many cannot afford to retain a lawyer.[148] Accordingly, many children

----

146. Interview by the Lawyers Committee, Pretoria, March 1986.

147. Affidavit, Uitenhage, February 2, 1985.

148. An accused may apply for free legal aid, for which there is a means test, but the grant of aid is not automatic and many applicants are refused. Once again, most juveniles have never heard of free legal aid and do not

charged with public violence appear in court without any legal representation, and must try to navigate the complex technicalities of the criminal procedure in defending themselves against serious charges.

This undoubtedly has severe consequences. The offense of public violence carries a potential jail sentence of between one and five years or more, depending on the seriousness of the activity and aggravating factors, such as whether the acts were planned, caused bodily injury or were directed against the security forces. According to a number of attorneys representing clients charged with public violence, sentencing tends to be much lighter when the accused has a lawyer, and there is a high rate of acquittals or withdrawal of charges in public violence cases where defendants are represented by counsel.[149] Two attorneys in Johannesburg who have handled numerous public violence cases estimate that approximately 90% of their cases have resulted in an acquittal or withdrawal of charges.[150]

Obtaining counsel provides no assurance of fair procedure, however. Attorneys representing children charged with public violence report that their work is often hampered by the police, who sometimes refuse to tell attorneys where the accused are being detained. The police are also slow to make available to attorneys the charge sheets and copies of any statements or confessions made by the accused while in custody.

Access to detainees is often blocked long enough to allow police time to extract a confession by intimidation, threats and assault (see Chapter VII, *infra*). One attorney described a typical pattern:

> It is usually impossible for me to hear about cases in time to be present at the child's first court appearance, 48 hours after arrest.

----

even apply. See Children in Prison In South Africa, Fiona McLachlan, Institute of Criminology, University of Cape Town, September 1984, at 23.

149. Interviews by Helena Cook, Port Elizabeth and Johannesburg, November 1985.

150. Id.

When they come back to court two weeks later, invariably they have been forced to make statements and confessions. Most of the accused are routinely beaten and kicked around by the police.[151]

Another lawyer, who represented two 11 year-old boys charged with public violence told us:

I was not allowed to see either of the boys until they appeared in court for the first time. I never even received the charge sheet for one of them despite repeated requests to the police. Even if you are permitted to see clients in the police cells, they are usually too scared to say anything because you must be in sight and hearing of a police officer.[152]

Still, children who have no legal representation are in a worse position. The same lawyer explained:

Many children are still appearing in court every day without a lawyer. When children do not have legal representation they are often asked to plead right away. They do not understand what is going on at all, but once they have pleaded then they must either be convicted or acquitted -- charges cannot be withdrawn.[153]

3. Detention Pending Trial

Persons arrested on a charge of public violence must be brought before a magistrates court within 48 hours, and further detention must be pursuant to a court order. The 48-hour period excludes days on which the court is not sitting. If, therefore, an arrest is made on a Thursday or Friday, the child is detained over the weekend until the

----

151. Interview by Helena Cook, Johannesburg, November 22, 1985.

152. Interview by Helena Cook, Cape Town, November 19, 1985.

153. Id.

court sits again on Monday. Also, if the child is not granted bail at the first court appearance, he or she typically is taken back to the cells and remains in jail for the duration of the proceedings, which can take months, or until a subsequent bail application is granted.

At the first court appearance an application for bail for the child can be made. Without a lawyer, the child is at a severe disadvantage. He or she may not even understand that bail can be sought and, if the police contest it, bail is unlikely to be granted.

A special provision in the law states that juveniles may be released into the custody of their parents without the payment of bail.[154] This provision is generally applied when juveniles are accused of other criminal offenses, even serious ones. Yet it has been frequently ignored in public violence and unrest-related cases. Bail money, even for children, typically has been set at several hundred Rand, well beyond the means of most black parents. The law makes provisions for bail money to be put up by a third party.[155] However, when church groups began to assist in providing funds for bail in public violence cases, some magistrates refused to grant bail on the grounds that there would then be no incentive for the accused to appear for trial.[156]

Denial of bail has meant that innocent children have languished in prison for months on end, awaiting a resolution of their trial. In Johannesburg, an 11 year-old child, Fanie Goduka, was refused bail by magistrates on two occasions after he was arrested on July 11, 1985 and detained on a charge of public violence. An appeal before the Supreme Court was necessary before Fanie finally was released into the custody of his mother. By that time, the child had been in prison for 57 days. The "public violence" that Fanie was alleged to have committed, and which he denied, consisted of throwing stones at two unoccupied

----

154. Criminal Procedure Act 1977, Section 72(1)(b).

155. Id., Section 69.

156. Interview by Helena Cook, Johannesburg, November 22, 1985.

motor vehicles, damaging the windscreens and body work. Incredibly, a police warrant officer asserted at the bail hearing that he believed Fanie would interfere with witnesses if released, and one of the magistrates who refused bail explained that the 11 year-old might be induced to flee the country.[157] When the case finally was heard in mid-January 1986, six months after his arrest, Fanie was acquitted of all charges.

In Middelburg magistrates court, an eight year-old boy, Amos Khubheka, was refused bail when he appeared without legal representation on a charge of intimidation in February 1986. Amos was arrested while playing outside his house when police came by in pursuit of some youths. His aunt reported that when she went with Amos's father to the police station the day he was arrested, the boy "was frantic and crying."[158] After DPSC lodged strong protests against the young child's continued detention, Amos was finally released a day after his court appearance.

On January 13, 1986 an urgent bail application on behalf of ten children, including a 14 year-old, and two adults was turned down after the state maintained that its investigation was not complete. Five of the accused had been fired upon by police; three had sustained birdshot injuries. One of the injured was still in the hospital at the time the application was brought. The others had already been in custody for one to two weeks.[159]

Even if released on bail, children sometimes are harassed and intimidated by police. One 14 year-old boy arrested in Mamelodi in December 1985 told his attorneys that, before his release, the police had threatened him with death if he were released. In mid-February 1986, two weeks after he was granted bail, the boy was shot dead by a policeman's son. According to witnesses, the shooting was "in cold blood" and "entirely unprovoked." The police have

----

157. Fanie Goduka v. The State, September 5, 1985. Interview by Helena Cook, Johannesburg, November 25, 1985.

158. "Eight-year-old refused bail," Weekly Mail, February 7-13, 1986.

159. "Children Refused Bail," Cape Times, January 14, 1986.

not yet laid any charges in respect of the killing.[160] The
other 17 arrested with the victim, all charged with the
murder of the policeman, have been consistently harrassed
by uniformed officers. Five of their homes have been
petrol-bombed in circumstances that point to police
involvement.

4. Trial Proceedings

Public violence cases are generally heard in the
regional magistrates' courts, lower courts that have both civil
and criminal jurisdiction. In criminal matters regional
magistrates are limited to imposing a maximum sentence of
10 years' imprisonment, a fine of R10,000 or a whipping.
Unlike judges in the higher courts (who are chosen from the
ranks of senior practicing lawyers), magistrates are public
servants appointed by the Minister of Justice who perform
both judicial and administrative functions. They are
overwhelmingly white, and their lack of independence from
the executive has long been the subject of a great deal of
criticism.

The huge numbers of public violence prosecutions
have placed an enormous strain on the magistrates' courts,
with the result that, in some areas, one or two magistrates
have been designated to hear only public violence or unrest-
related cases. The same policemen frequently appear as
prosecution witnesses in many of these cases. In these
circumstances it is not surprising that some magistrates have,
according to attorneys, demonstrated a bias toward the
prosecution.

Sentencing in public violence cases has been very
severe, even for children with no previous criminal record.
Some magistrates have indicated that harsh sentences were
intended to discourage further incidents of unrest.
Sentencing has been particularly heavy in areas where
popular resistance and opposition is strong, and where unrest
has been severe and prolonged, such as the Eastern Cape. In
that area typical sentences, even for throwing a stone, have
been between three and seven years imprisonment. This is

----

160. Interview by the Lawyers Committee, Pretoria, March 26, 1986.

irrespective of whether the accused is a juvenile or a first offender.[161]

Many public violence cases and related offenses have been prosecuted on extremely insubstantial or questionable evidence, and some children have reported that the evidence against them was fabricated by the police. Fifteen year-old Jerry was arrested in June 1985 on his way to visit a family whose child had been killed by the police. Jerry and his friends noticed two police land-rovers coming towards them and they started to run away. Jerry said:

> [T]hey caught me, one of them hit me with a brick on the head. They took us to Wynberg police station. When we arrived they said I have beat them with a brick.[162]

Jerry was detained on a public violence charge in Diepkloof prison for a month. He was beaten up during interrogation and was released eventually.

In Mamelodi, Adam, a 14 year-old boy, was arrested on September 23, 1985 with 17 others on charges of public violence and related criminal offenses arising out of the burning of a policeman's house. According to their attorney, many of the accused were not even in the township when the alleged offenses occurred and they do not know one another. The sole common factor among them is that they all are members of the student organization COSAS. Adam was detained until November 26, when he was released on bail. [163]

----

161. In July 1985, a magistrate in Uitenhage sentenced an 18 year-old youth, Zolisile Ndwanya, to a total of 26 years imprisonment on seven counts of public violence. Three of the sentences were to run concurrently, reducing the jail term to an effective 12 years. In passing sentence, the magistrate said this type of offense was very prevalent and referred to the damage which had been caused by the unrest. Zolisile was a first offender. "Unrest Crimes: Youth jailed for 12 years," Evening Post, July 11, 1985.

162. Statement, Johannesburg, January 1986.

163. On December 12, 1985 he was again arrested with four of his brothers and sisters in connection with a robbery that took place on October 20, 1985, while Adam was in custody. Both cases have been postponed

In another case in Leandra, five boys, two aged 15 years and the others only 12, 13 and 14 years old, were accused of malicious damage to property in respect of an offense they were alleged to have committed two days after their arrest when they were already in the police cells.[164] One attorney noted that such inconsistencies and inaccuracies in police evidence often emerge only on cross-examination, which underscores the advisability of legal representation.

In a case before the Soweto magistrates' courts on November 28, 1985, three boys, two aged 17 years and the other 15, appeared in the dock. The prosecutor wanted to ask for a further remand because two of his witnesses (members of the SADF) had not appeared at the court. Defense counsel resisted since the arrests were made in July and the case already had been remanded three times. Eventually, the case proceeded. The evidence of the single white soldier present was simple, if unexpected. He had not actually seen the boys doing anything, he said, but had been told to arrest them by his superiors. The three accused were speedily acquitted.[165]

The insufficiency of much of the evidence often results in repeated requests for postponements by the prosecution, which almost invariably are granted. According to an attorney in Pretoria, postponements requested by the defense are met with extreme hostility by the court and generally are denied.[166] The repeated court appearances increase the legal fees, and some parents have lost their jobs because they have had to attend court with their child so frequently. These postponements also prolong the time that an accused who has been denied bail must remain in custody. Seventeen year-old Isaac Clifton spent 18 months

----

repeatedly at the request of the prosecution. Adam has now appeared in court 13 times in respect of these charges.Interview by the Lawyers Committee, Pretoria, March 26, 1985.

164. State vs. Aaron Mavusa, Johannesburg, 1985.

165. Case observed by Helena Cook, Soweto Magistrates' Court, November 28, 1985.

166. Interview by the Lawyers Committee, Pretoria, March 26, 1986.

in detention before being acquitted of charges of murder and subversion. Isaac was shot in the leg by police on September 4, 1984 as he was on his way to the store. He was told to run home but, two weeks later, the police came back and arrested him. He said:

> I think there must have been a presumption that because I stay in the same street as the murdered councillor, Jacob Chakare, and had a bullet wound in the leg, I must have been shot at the scene of the murder.

Isaac was held in custody while the case was repeatedly remanded at the request of the prosecution. He was eventually acquitted after 18 months in jail. "When I was acquitted I didn't know whether to cry or not," he said. "I feel bitter that so much of my time has been wasted."[167]

In another case in Mamelodi, 18 juveniles were arrested in early December 1985 and charged with murder after the death of a policeman in the township. Bail was refused and the prosecution attempted to postpone the court hearing twice, going ahead only after the defense lawyer threatened to make an urgent application to the Supreme Court. The hearing finally commenced on January 24, 1986. The State's cross-examination lasted until January 30. On that day, half way through defense counsel's cross-examination of the investigating police officer, the witness failed to return after lunch, although he was later seen conversing with the prosecution counsel[168].

C. Arrest Under the Emergency Regulations

According to recent government statistics, some 2106 children under the age of 16 were arrested and detained under the emergency regulations in less than seven months

----

167. "Back to Class -- After Eighteen Months in Police Cells," Weekly Mail, February 28 - March 6, 1986.

168. Interview by the Lawyers Committee, Pretoria, March 26, 1986.

between July 21, 1985 and January 31, 1986.[169]   These
figures are an indication of the large-scale arrests of
children that took place during the State of Emergency, but
it is practically impossible to calculate exactly how many of
the 7996 emergency detainees were children under the age
of 18. The Detainees' Parents Support Committee (DPSC)
estimated in October 1985 that 60% of the 5,000 or so
emergency detainees held at that time were under 25 years
old, and 23% were under 15 years old.

Although the police clearly targeted for arrest
children whom they believed to be active in various youth
organizations, many of the arrests under the emergency
regulations, particularly of younger children, appear to have
been random and indiscriminate, with little or no evidence
that the child was involved in any activity relating to the
unrest. Since the emergency regulations did not require that
any charges be filed, they enabled police to arrest children
on the streets, in schools and in their homes for no apparent
reason.

The extended powers of arrest and detention under
the emergency regulations provided that any member of the
security forces could arrest anyone without a warrant if, in
his opinion, this was necessary for "the maintenance of
public order or the safety of the public or that person
himself, or for the termination of the state of emergency."
Once someone -- including a child -- was arrested, he or
she could be detained without charge for up to 14 days, and
thereafter indefinitely by order of the Minister of Law and
Order, as long as the State of Emergency remained in effect.
The regulations expressly excluded any right of the detainee
to receive notice that his detention had been extended or to
be given an opportunity to make representations to the
Minister concerning his detention. Any member of the
security forces also had the right to interrogate a person so
arrested or detained.

Emergency detainees were subject to a strict code of
discipline. A wide range of offenses, including insolence,

----

169. Statistics supplied in response to a Parliamentary question during the
    1986 session and published in the Weekly Mail, February 28-March 6,
    1986.

idleness, singing, whistling and conversing with another detainee without permission, were punishable by solitary confinement, deprivation of food, corporal punishment or a fine.

It was extremely difficult to ensure the safety and well-being of children arrested and detained under the emergency regulations. Emergency detainees were not allowed access to anyone, including a lawyer, without special permission, which was frequently denied.[170]

It was practically impossible to challenge detentions in court because the emergency regulations expressly indemnified the security forces against any legal proceedings for all acts carried out "in good faith" during the emergency ("good faith" to be presumed until the contrary was proved).[171]

In some cases police were slow to confirm a child's detention. On occasion, the police even denied that they were holding a child in custody, and the detention became known only when fellow detainees were released.

The emergency regulations suggest that this form of detention was intended to be a form of preventive detention of persons believed to be involved in perpetrating the unrest. In fact, arrests of children were so numerous and often so arbitrary that it seems that emergency arrests and detentions were frequently used simply to terrorize children and to act as a deterrent to others.

In many cases the police made little attempt to question an emergency detainee about his or her possible involvement in incidents of unrest. Some detainees have said that they were perfunctorily questioned about their political affiliations and their friends, while others were not questioned at all. Also, a number of young emergency detainees were simply released after the initial period of 14 days, or even earlier, suggesting that there was no basis on

----

170. Interviews by Helena Cook, Johannesburg and Cape Town, November 1985.

171. Emergency Regulations, section 11.

which the Minister of Law and Order could have authorized the detention to be prolonged beyond this time.

The principal of a school in Orlando East described how one of his 12 year-old pupils, Joe, was picked up by a policeman on August 21, 1985 as the child was on his way to school, wearing school uniform and carrying a bag of books. Joe was taken to a police station with a number of other young children:

> They were put in cells. They were given food twice a day. There were many other boys in the cell and they slept two to each bed. On Friday afternoon at about 3 p.m. they were again put into a hippo [armored military vehicle] and each boy and girl was delivered to his or her home. They were not told why they had been arrested.[172]

An 11 year-old girl at the same school was picked up two days later on her way home and was held overnight in the police cells, with no explanation, with a number of other children. They were given no food and were released early the next day.[173] Young children who have been held in police cells like this for only a few hours or one or two days often were not included in the police lists of emergency detainees. This means that the official statistics of emergency detainees under-represent the actual number of children who have gone through the experience of being arrested and locked up in a cell, often with no idea why they were there or when they would be released.

The huge increase in arrests and detention without charge during the State of Emergency led to mounting criticism from concerned groups such as the DPSC, particularly with respect to the arrests and detention of very young children, and finally prompted a reaction from the South African government. In December 1985, Mr. Ismail, a former detainee held under the emergency regulations who had shared a cell with some children in Victor Verster

----

172. Report of school principal, Orlando East, August 26, 1985.

173. Id.

prison in the Western Cape, placed an advertisement in a Cape Town newspaper calling for the release of all children in detention under 16 years old. Mr. Ismail claimed that children as young as eight years old had been detained, and that one of the 14 year-old boys in his cell (who was then still in detention) was in great distress.

The Minister of Law and Order immediately telexed the newspaper, stating that any children under 16 "had long been released following requests made to me by Judges Munnik and Friedman." There were in fact at least five boys under 16 still detained under the emergency regulations in Victor Verster prison at the time the Minister made this statement. Two of them had been held for more than 36 days. Their detention would, in accordance with the regulations, have to have been specifically authorized by the Minister himself.

When questioned about this, the Minister replied that he had been referring only to Cape Town itself and not to Boland, where the prison is located. Yet Mr. Ismail's advertisement was clearly referring to Victor Verster prison, where he and most of the other black male emergency detainees were held. Forced to admit the continued detention of the boys, a police liaison officer said that their cases were "receiving urgent attention." Nevertheless, it was another three weeks before four of the boys were finally released on December 24, 1985.[174]

On a radio broadcast in early December the Minister also said that, as a matter of policy, young children were released into the care of their parents as quickly as possible and that the police tried not to detain children under 16 longer than necessary.[175] Despite this, children under 16 continued to be detained. On December 25, 1985, for example, shortly after the Minister's statement, two children from Paarl, aged 13 and 14, were arrested and detained in Victor Verster prison under the emergency regulations. It was reported that eight other schoolboys, including a ten

----

174. "Children are being held in prison," Cape Times, December 7, 1985.

175. "Le Grange denial on children," Cape Times, December 6, 1985.

year-old, were being held, although the police would not officially confirm this.[176]

D. Informing Parents

Children who are arrested are made still more vulnerable by the pervasive failure of police to notify parents of a child's arrest. Parents who were not present at the time of arrest typically have no idea what has become of their child unless they are informed by someone who saw or heard about it. Once a child has "disappeared" it is now common for parents to embark on a horrific search, going from police stations to prisons to hospitals and finally to the mortuaries. The police sometimes add to the trauma by denying that a child they are holding is in detention.

When Mrs. Sekgatle's 15 year-old daughter, Rebecca, was arrested under the emergency regulations as she left the dentist's clinic, Mrs. Sekgatle visited numerous prisons and police stations on the East Rand, Vereeniging, the West Rand and, finally, Johannesburg's Diepkloof prison before locating her daughter. Even then she was not allowed to see Rebecca as she did not have the required permit.[177]

Three groups working closely with detainees and especially children, Lawyers for Human Rights, Child Welfare and DPSC, have said they have never come across a single case where a parent has been informed of the child's detention by police. Children interviewed by the Lawyers Committee for Human Rights who were arrested in the absence of their parents stated that their parents were never officially informed of the child's detention. Yet, when this problem was raised by the Committee of Concern for Children, the Minister of Law and Order replied, "I am not aware of any instance where members of the South African

----

176. "Two boys aged 13 and 14 detained," Cape Times, January 1, 1985 and "Boy, 14, detained," Cape Times, January 11, 1986.

177. "Where has my little girl Rebecca gone?" The Sowetan, August 20, 1985. Visitors' permits are discussed under 'Access to Detainees,' Chapter XI.B, infra.

police failed to inform parents of the detention or whereabouts of their children."[178]

Many parents of children arrested on criminal charges have not even been told of the time or place of the child's scheduled appearance in court, despite the fact that the law requires that the parent or guardian be notified of any court proceedings involving a juvenile.[179] Parents are compelled to go from one police station to another to inquire whether their child is there or to spend long hours in the magistrates' courts waiting to see if their child makes an appearance.

The police have contributed to the confusion and lack of information about children who have been arrested. They are slow to confirm detentions, alleging lack of manpower, though they repeatedly send out squads of police to effect one arrest. Some children reported that the police took down their names inaccurately and recorded their ages as being higher than they actually were, particularly in the case of children under 16 years old. When desperate parents seek the assistance of groups such as Black Sash and DPSC in tracing a child, the police generally refuse to respond to these groups and threaten people with harassment if they seek such assistance.

----

178. Letter from Minister dated October 14, 1985 addressed to the chairman of the Committee of Concern for Children, Linksfield, S.A.

179. Criminal Procedure Act, Section 74(1). The only exception that the section provides is if the parent is not in the magisterial district or cannot be traced without "undue delay." A recent study of children in prisons in South Africa noted that, if the legislature had intended that this provision ensure that parents were present when their child appeared in court, it had "failed dramatically." It found, as well, that magistrates "very readily accepted the absence of parents without further investigation." Also, by virtue of the afore-mentioned statutory provision, if the court is in a white area and the accused is black, the Act itself provides "an easy, yet perfectly legal means of securing the child's attendance without his/her parent(s)." Children In Prisons in South Africa Fiona McLachlan, University of Cape Town, September 1984 at 24.

CHAPTER VII

Assault and Torture of Children in Detention

Severe torture and assaults are routinely inflicted on political detainees in South Africa, and children have not been spared. Security laws that permit lengthy detention without charge provide both an invitation to abuse, and a shield from public scrutiny.

The torture of detainees in South Africa has been well documented. In a 1984 report,[180] Amnesty International found "considerable evidence to show that political detainees were commonly tortured and ill-treated during interrogation by security police." Most of the victims were uncharged detainees held in solitary confinement for interrogation under the security legislation.

In 1982, the Detainees' Parents Support Committee (DPSC) issued a report based on interviews with 70 former detainees. The report concluded that "systematic and widespread torture is an integral feature of the detention system."[181]

A recent report by the University of Cape Town (UCT) found that torture is a routine feature of interrogation during detention. [182] The report was based on interviews with 176 former security detainees, 83% of whom claimed they had suffered some form of physical abuse; all claimed to have been subjected to psychologial coercion. Broken down according to race, evidence of torture was highest among Africans (93% claiming some form of abuse), who were also "apparently far more heavily tortured and subjected to far more violent forms of psychological coercion than white detainees." The report noted that

----

180. Torture In The Eighties, Amnesty International, 1984.

181. Memorandum on Security Police Abuses of Political Detainees, DPSC, September 1982.

182. A Study of Detention and Torture in South Africa: Preliminary Report, Don Foster and Diane Sandler, Institute of Criminology, University of Cape Town, September 1985.

detention, as "a closed system, with detainees almost entirely in the hands of the security police," was psychologically "severely debilitating."

Broadly speaking, the most common abuses against detainees, as described in both the DPSC and UCT reports, include electric shock; beating; enforced standing and exercise; severe food and sleep deprivation; the so-called "helicopter," in which the victim is handcuffed at the wrists and ankles and suspended over a pole between two chairs, sometimes for hours, while being severely beaten and interrogated; suffocation; enforced nakedness; shackling; prolonged interrogation; and humiliation and threats.

Such torture is hardly a new phenomenon. Indeed, all but four of the detainees in the UCT survey had been detained between 1974 and 1983 -- before the current unrest had really taken hold. However, allegations of the widespread and severe torture of security detainees began to surface with increasing frequency as the unrest escalated. Since emergency detainees generally were not totally isolated during their detention (unlike ISA detainees held in solitary confinement), reports of this torture taking place began to emerge while the victims were still in custody.

A. Assault At the Time of Arrest

Children who have been arrested are routinely subjected to physical assault by the security forces at the time of arrest and in the early stages of custody. Such assaults typically occur when the arrest is made, inside the police or SADF vehicles on the way to a police station, and in the police cells in the initial hours or days of detention before the child is moved to a prison. These attacks commonly involve punching, kicking, slapping, whipping or beating with rifle butts and other heavy objects. A number of children have sustained broken teeth and bones, perforated eardrums and other serious injuries as a result of such assaults.

Three young boys in Dobsonville, two aged 13 and one only 11 years old, were arrested on November 8, 1985 when police came to break up a crowd attending a night vigil for a 15 year-old boy killed by the security forces. Tear gas was fired into the house and inside a tent that had been erected for the mourners. The police kicked down the doors and began assaulting people in the house. The 11 year-old boy was picked up and flung against a wall by a policeman.[183]

Everyone in the house was forced to get into waiting police vans. According to the boys, the security forces formed two lines between which people had to pass to reach the vans. As they passed, they were hit with sjamboks and fists and were kicked. At the police station they were again beaten with sjamboks and fists. The 11 year-old boy sustained three broken teeth. The sjambokking left wounds on the bodies of all three boys; one had a badly swollen and cut lip, and another was left with swollen and bruised eyes. All three were held for three days. When the police finally asked how old they were, they were released. They were told to leave the police station, which was located several miles from their homes. Their parents were not notified and they had no money. Finally, they hitched a lift home on a garbage truck. The police later denied having any record of their detention.

Sixteen year-old Ashraf Mahomed was arrested for questioning in early February 1985 at 5:30 in the morning. According to his mother's affidavit, when police forced Ashraf into the waiting van, "they deliberately smashed his head on the side of the vehicle." Charged with public violence, Ashraf was released on bail and bore "visible signs of sjambokking on his back and on his legs." He complained that police "had hit him all over his body."[184]

Ditwe, aged 15, was arrested at his home in Motetema at 5 a.m. on October 9, 1985. The police wanted him to tell them the names of students who had been causing disturbances at Ditwe's school. At the police station Ditwe was kicked, punched and whipped until he bled. In the course of the assault, both of his arms were fractured

----

183. Interview by Dayle Powell, Johannesburg, November 1985.

184. Affidavit of Zuleikha Fakier Mahomed in Wendy Orr and Others v. The Minister of Law and Order and Others, September 25, 1985.

and the wrist joints deformed. He was not permitted to see a doctor for the five days that he remained in custody. On his release, he spent five days in a hospital, where he was treated for deep slash wounds left by a sjambok on his chest and back. Both of his arms were encased in plaster.[185]

A woman from Alexandra who was detained in Diepkloof prison for three months stated that, on October 9, 1985, she saw 14 girls between nine and 15 years old being brought into the prison. The girls were badly bruised, and told her that they had been arrested and taken to Moroka police station for the night. They said that during the night the riot squad police had assaulted them with heavy whips.[186]

The experiences of four boys arrested in January and February 1986 are typical. Thabo, aged 17, was arrested on February 6, 1986 while he was at a friend's house. The police broke down the door and beat Thabo with canes and sjamboks. Thabo was taken to the police station where he was beaten again by "a mob of policemen" with sjamboks. He was then taken before another police officer, who made him strip naked and beat him on his genitals with a sjambok so badly that he later had one testicle removed.[187]

In Diepkloof, on January 25, 1986, Vincent, aged 14, was walking home when he was stopped by police and asked for the names of some of the young activists in the township. When he said he did not know, the police accused him of stoning a car and arrested him. Vincent recalled that "they started beating me with a sjambok and a black man came in and started beating me up with fists and he also kicked me."[188] Two days later he was released without being charged.

Martin and Steven were both arrested and accused of stoning a vehicle. Martin stated, "I was beaten with a gun

----

185. Statement, Johannesburg, October 25, 1985.

186. Statement, Johannesburg, October 18, 1985.

187. Statement, Pretoria, February 1986.

188. Statement, Johannesburg, January 30, 1986.

butt on the mouth by a white policeman. Two of my front teeth were broken."[189] According to Steven:

> They started sjambokking me all over the body. I fell down and they started kicking me all over while I was lying down. I stood up and he sjambokked me on the left ear. I was bleeding profusely by then. We were never taken to a doctor.[190]

The boys were beaten again when they were taken into the hippo and yet again at Randburg police station. "They showed us two bricks and said we should admit that we were stoning the vehicle. When we refused they would beat us." Martin finally said the bricks were theirs. He later explained, "There was nothing we could do, they were beating us left and right. I was bleeding on my left eye."

A number of children arrested and charged with public violence, like Martin and Steven, report that they were assaulted in order to compel them to sign a statement admitting to the alleged offenses. By law, confessions are admissable in court as proof of guilt only if made freely and reduced to writing in the presence of a magistrate or judge. Another provision of the Criminal Procedure Act, however, eviscerates this supposed protection, allowing certain information given in court by a police witness, even though discovered only by means of an otherwise inadmissible confession, to be admitted at criminal proceedings.[191] It appears that police have taken full advantage of the license thus accorded them to extract confessions from children. Children arrested for public violence have described brutal interrogations at police stations:[192]

----

189. Statement, Johannesburg, 1986.

190. Statement, Johannesburg, 1986.

191. Criminal Procedure Act, sections 217 and 218.

192. The statements from which the following extracts come were taken by attorneys representing children on charges of public violence in Johannesburg and Pretoria during 1985.

- 105 -

S. called me to his office. He asked me if I
threw stones at SM's house, I said no, I was
at home.   S. punched me, left me in the
office and called B. B. placed [a] white sack
over my head and I was taken to another
room.   I was alone, tear gas [was] sprayed, I
screamed [and I was] taken out back to S.'s
office.   [I was] asked if I threw stones.   I
denied.   S. put the sack on and I was
shocked. I then agreed that I threw stones

JM (aged 17).

* * * *

. . . they put a sack on my face choking me
and tear gassing to [get me to] admit that I
stoned a house of M . . . . Then they forced
me to admit and write a statement . . . .
Mr., he handcuffed me on a seat and choked
me till I admit[ted this] . . . . On the very
same day ([the] 19th) we appeared at court
with two white policeman who forced us to
admit, we then admit[ted] only because those
policemen were there . . . .

AK (aged 17).

* * * *

They pulled me out of the van and took me
to a room where they threw [sic] me and
opened tear gas and closed the room. They
opened tear gas for three times after every 5
minutes. At 8 a.m. the same morning, I was
taken to Mr. S. He cross questioned me and
every time I was beaten up by the other
white policeman.   I was bleeding from the
nose . . . . I was kept there till Friday . . . .
I was told to go home . . . . [t]he white
policemen told me that if they can find me in
the street or attending any meeting they will
shoot me and I'll be killed.

JM (aged 17)

* * * *

We were made to face the wall in the charge office and repeatedly beaten with sjamboks .
. . . I was then interrogated alone and assaulted in the following manner:

       a. M. handcuffed me to a wooden chair;

       b. I was repeatedly assaulted with a sjambok
           and fists by [three policemen] .
. . .

The assault was furious:

I had sjambok marks all over my body and was covered in blood. My forehead was swollen from where [I was struck] with a sjambok on my head. Because of my injuries, I was taken from [interrogation] room 9 and placed in a [van]. I could not walk to the [van] and had to be dragged. While I was in the [van], a number of other people were taken individually into room 9. I heard [them] screaming.

CC (aged 17).

* * * *

While we were waiting [a policeman] kicked me on the mouth; (another policeman) struck me with a wire coat hanger. He also pulled the coat hanger through my hair causing me considerable pain . . . . I was taken for interrogation. I was told to take off my clothes, and I was asked questions . . . . I was assaulted . . . as follows:

a. the short policeman burnt
my hair with a cigarette
lighter;

b. a tube was pulled over my
mouth and I was electrocuted
on my back;

c. the short white policeman
hit me with a hosepipe on my
fingers.

RM (aged 15).

In addition to physical assault, children report that
the police use threats as another means of intimidation. A 16
year-old boy arrested in Mohlakeng on October 20, 1985,
was interrogated about incidents of stone throwing. He said,
"Colonel Viljoen told me that I would be going to jail for
life."[193]   Children have also been threatened with death.
When riots broke out in Alexandra on February 5, 1986,
Abraham, aged 16, was arrested when police found him in
possession of a list of names of the dead, injured and
missing in the township during the riots.   Abraham was
beaten and kicked and told by his interrogator to confess to
the burning of a policeman, "or he would hang me in the
cell until I died." Abraham said:

I broke down and wept. I was then ordered to
lie down spreadeagled and . . . [a policeman]
came in and put his foot on my genitals and
said I should own up to the killing . . . . then
a [policeman] pointed a gun under my chin
and said that if I didn't confess and identify
others that he would kill me.[194]

Such abuse has led to the arrest of still more children
who were not even involved in incidents of unrest. Police
have made arrests on the basis of information forcibly
obtained from other detainees.   Some young "informers"

----

193. Statement, Johannesburg, December 1985.

194. Affidavit, Alexandra, February 23, 1986.

have later admitted that they gave any names they could think of because they were frightened of what might happen to them if they refused. Sarah, arrested in Bellville on September 5, 1985, described such an experience:

> We were taken to a room in the police station where all the police were drinking coffee. A policeman said that we should be given pages to write down the names of those who had thrown stones. I was very afraid and began to write down any names I could think of. When I couldn't remember any more one policeman hit me hard with an orange sjambok. I was just putting down any names that came into my head because I was so afraid. They then asked who had been burning tyres. I was told to give names and addresses . . . . [None] of the people I named had to my knowledge been involved in these offenses or anything illegal.[195]

Despite the severity and pervasiveness of this type of abuse, it has received little attention. Legislative efforts to introduce safeguards for detainees ensuring that they are regularly visited and have access to medical assistance have focused on the prisons, and do not extend to police cells. Also, these provisions apply only to security detainees and not to those held on criminal charges. As noted earlier, these safeguards rarely offer effective protection from police abuse but they do at least indicate some recognition of the problem.

B. Abuse of Children in Detention

Torture of detainees is pervasive in South Africa's prisons, and young children number among the victims. Though torture has long been inflicted upon political prisoners in South Africa, the practice claimed greater public attention during the State of Emergency. As noted earlier, unlike detainees held pursuant to the ISA,

----

195. Affidavit, Cape Town, September 18, 1985.

emergency detainees generally were not held in solitary confinement. This allowed reports of their torture to emerge while the victims were still detained.

The widespread allegations of torture of emergency detainees prompted a series of applications to the South African courts seeking an urgent interdict[196] to prevent police from further assaulting victims while they remained in detention. These, in turn, served to focus still greater attention on the practice. A number of these interdicts were granted. It has been much more difficult to take legal action in respect of the torture of ISA detainees, who are held incommunicado and can be detained until all physical marks of abuse have healed.

The interdict application that attracted the most attention was filed in Port Elizabeth on September 25, 1985 by a young district surgeon, Dr. Wendy Orr, and 43 others. Several of the detainees on whose behalf this application was made were under the age of 18. More than 200 pages of affidavit evidence were placed before the court, and resulted in a far-reaching order by Mr. Justice Eksteen. The order enjoined the South African Police from assaulting or threatening to assault not only the detainees on whose behalf the application had been brought, but all present and future detainees at the St. Albans and North End prisons in Port Elizabeth.[197] The scope of this order was particularly significant in light of DPSC statistics that indicate that the highest number of emergency detentions (42.8%) occurred in the Eastern Cape area where Port Elizabeth is situated.

When the application was filed, Wendy Orr was a district surgeon whose duties included the medical examination of emergency detainees. In her affidavit she alleged that large numbers of the detainees she examined complained of assault and showed symptoms consistent with their complaints. According to her affidavit:

----

196. This legal remedy is similar to an interim injunction and is granted where a prima facie case establishing the urgency of a remedy is made out, pending full argument of the case. At least 17 such applications were made during 1985 (Weekly Mail, February 21-27, 1986).

197. Wendy Orr and others v. The Minister of Law and Order and others, South Eastern Cape Local Division, September 25, 1985.

They had weals, bruising, blisters over their backs, arms and on the palms of their hands. Some had lacerated lips and the skin over their cheekbones was split. Several had had their eardrums perforated.

She examined several detainees with "unusual injuries consistent with an assault on a restrained victim." At least 48 had "such a multiplicity of injuries they could not have been inflicted during the course of arrest."

Dr. Orr concluded that assaults of detainees were taking place on a "massive scale" and that the police, apparently believing themselves to be protected by the indemnity in the emergency regulations, considered they were not accountable. At the same time, the Departments of Prisons and Health had "turned a blind eye" to what was happening in the prisons.

Dr. Orr's efforts to expose police abuse of detainees were severely hampered. According to her evidence, after she began to express concern about the magnitude and frequency of assault, the prison medical records of certain patients she had examined, who had been particularly badly assaulted, disappeared. She also stated that, "I received instructions not to endorse the medical records requesting an investigation of the alleged assaults." Shortly after the court application was filed, Dr. Orr was relieved of her prison duties. She eventually gave up her post as district surgeon altogether.

One of the children on whose behalf the Port Elizabeth application was brought was 16 year-old Ashraf Mohamed. Ashraf was arrested on four occasions in 1985, and alleged that he was tortured during each episode. The first assault, described in Section A, *supra*, took place at the time of arrest. The others occurred while Ashraf was detained.

The second arrest took place on July 31 and was effected pursuant to the emergency regulations. A week later, when Ashraf's parents visited him, "he kept holding his stomach and complained of a pain in his ribs, head and stomach. He also had bruises under his eyes."[198]

Ashraf was released on August 14, and was again arrested under the emergency regulations only nine days later. Upon his release on September 5:

> Ashraf said that his ears, hand and back were very painful and that he had been blindfolded during his detention, that his head had been covered with a wet bag and that he was given electric shocks. He said that when they had finished shocking him they tied him to a chair and beat him about the ears for a prolonged period. The only medication he was given was a packet of aspirins. We examined him and noticed that he had recently healed burn marks on his hands and bruise marks on his eyes. In addition his nose was swollen.[199]

Only six days after this release, Ashraf was arrested for the fourth time. This time the family were denied all access to him. Since they had been granted permits to visit during Ashraf's previous periods in detention, his mother feared that they were now being refused a permit because Ashraf had been so badly assaulted that the police did not want anyone to see him. A number of other parents who joined the Port Elizabeth application had also been denied permission to visit their children, and also feared that their children had been assaulted.

Another urgent application to prevent further assault was brought in Grahamstown. One of the applicants in that case, Andrew, is only 12 years old. Andrew was arrested on September 6, 1985 and detained in connection with the death of a black policeman in the township. Andrew stated in his affidavit:

----

198. Id., Affidavit of Zuleikha Fakier Mahomed.

199. Id.

At the [CID] offices, I was assaulted by Constable TSWELE and Constable MGEBUZA, who struck me with clenched fists and kicked me . . . . I was assaulted by white policemen who beat me with a sjambok and cane on my back. I am unable to state how many blows were struck in that I was terrified . . . . I was not assaulted continuously, but at intervals.[200]

A 16 year-old detainee, Zukizani, also arrested in connection with the policeman's death and held in the same cell as Andrew, stated:

[P]olicemen took hold of me and lifted me off the ground and allowed me to drop to the floor while holding my legs and arms. This was repeated several times and during this process, while I was on the ground, [a policeman] stood on my stomach . . . . I recall screaming.[201]

While Zukizani and Andrew were in the police cells with four other detainees, three police constables came into the cell with canes and a sjambok:

We were made to bend down and [were] caned on the buttocks . . . . We were also required to do exercises . . . . When we tired and were unable to do the exercises to the satisfaction of the aforesaid police, we were struck by means of the canes and sjambok . . . . Constable Roberts struck me on the head with a sjambok causing an open wound which bled . . . . Before they left, we were informed that it was their intention to return later that night at which time we could expect a sound beating.[202]

----

200. Affidavit, Grahamstown, September 1985.

201. Sworn affidavit, Grahamstown, September 1985.

202. Id.

Zukizani also describes how police placed a rope around the neck of one of the detainees and "attempted to suspend him from the cell door by passing the rope over the door and pulling from the other side. When [he] screamed, they stopped."[203] The forced exercises and beatings were repeated at 11 p.m. that night and again the following night at 10 p.m.

A third detainee in the cell, Pinky, who is 15 years old, was also assaulted when he arrived at the police station for questioning:

> Sergeant Spence hit me with a stick on [my] upper arms and lower leg. [A policeman] hit me with his clenched fists on the bridge of my nose. I was also slapped.[204]

All three boys were questioned about the policeman's death. They claimed the police threatened that they would be made to experience the pain that the dead man had suffered. Twelve year-old Andrew had a tyre placed around his neck and the police threatened to set fire to it.[205] The other two became "upset and distressed" when they were taken to the mortuary and were forced to view and touch the "charred and incinerated" body of the policeman.

Some children have been subjected to more sophisticated forms of torture. A successful urgent application against further torture was brought in a Durban court on behalf of Eugene Vusi Dlamini in September 1985. Eugene is 16 years old and was arrested by about 20 policemen at his home at 6 a.m. on August 27, 1985 while he was getting ready for school. The police did not say why they were arresting Eugene, but his mother described how a man, whose face and head were hooded, pointed out Eugene

----

203. Id.

204. Affidavit, Grahamstown, September 1985.

205. The "necklace," as it has come to be known, has become a common form of summary killing in the townships of those suspected to be informers or collaborators. A tyre filled with petrol is put around the victim's neck and set alight. The police have begun to use this as a threat against detainees.

to the police at the time of the arrest. He was later interrogated about the activities of the United Democratic Front, the multi-racial non-parliamentary opposition coalition. The police told Mrs. Dlamini to "shut up" when she asked why her son was being arrested. The police searched the house and threatened another of her sons, who was sick, with a firearm. Mrs. Dlamini was not informed that Eugene was being arrested under Section 29 of the ISA (detention for the purposes of interrogation). Section 29 detainees can be held indefinitely in solitary confinement without charge until they have "responded to all questions satisfactorily."

Mrs. Dlamini next heard from her son one week later, on September 3, when he telephoned her from a hospital. She stated:

> At first, I did not realize that the person to whom I was speaking was [Eugene], because he appeared to speak with great difficulty and seemed to be under great stress . . . . In my conversation with him, he advised me as follows:
>
> (a) He was a patient at Shifa Hospital since Sunday, 1 September 1985.
>
> (b) He had been injured as a result of having been severely assaulted by the police from the time that he arrived at C.R. Swart Square Police Station.
>
> (c) He had been assaulted at various times at the Security Police premises and that, as a result, he was unable to hear properly in one ear, that his jaw bones were broken and that he suspected his forearms and skull were also broken.

(d) While he was at C.R. Swart Square the police interrogating him had given him wet blankets for use when he was to sleep.[206]

Eugene also told his mother that he feared further assaults by the police as soon as he was taken back to the police station. Mrs. Dlamini was never officially informed that her son was in the hospital and was due to undergo a series of operations for his serious condition. She brought an application before the Supreme Court to prevent further assault and to have Eugene fully examined by a doctor and a magistrate.

Eugene told the magistrate that on the day of his arrest he was "attacked" by six policemen at the station:

> [T]hey covered my face and mouth with a piece of tube. Then they kicked me in the stomach. They punched me in the stomach with clenched fists. I lost consciousness.[207]

He was then blindfolded and tied by both hands and feet to a chair:

> They poured water over my head and then over my feet. I then felt that they were shocking me . . . . Both my feet were shaking.[208]

The report of the district surgeon, carried out by order of the court, revealed that the surgeon had first examined Eugene at 4 p.m. on the day of his arrest. The report states:

----

206. Affidavit of Mrs. Doras Dlamini in the matter of <u>Doras Dlamini v. the Minister of Law and Order and the Commissioner of South African Police</u>, Durban, September 6, 1985.

207. Statement of Eugene Vusi Dlamini made under oath before Mr. K. A. Templeton, Senior Magistrate, September 18, 1985.

208. <u>Id</u>.

He was unable to talk at the time and indicated by signs and in writing that he had pain at the back of his throat, that his left ear was painful and that he had difficulty in closing his jaw. . . . He indicated areas at the base of the jaw on both sides of the upper neck anteriorly and alleged that he had been tied there with warm cloths.[209]

In addition, his tongue was swollen, the inside of his mouth was lacerated and his left ear was hemorrhaging.

Eugene said that he had vomited practically all night. The next day he was taken back to the interrogation room and made to stand against the wall with his hands behind his head:

They kicked and punched me in the stomach and told me to tell the truth. This proceeded for about three hours. They took it in turns.[210]

When the district surgeon saw Eugene the following day, he found further evidence of assault consistent with Eugene's account. He also found that Eugene had been kicked in the chest that morning and that his left eardrum was perforated.[211] The injuries were so severe that an ear, nose and throat specialist was called to examine Eugene on August 31.

During the next few days, Eugene was interrogated repeatedly. He was forced to crouch practically naked for two hours, after which he was strapped on his back to a table, doused with water and subjected to more electric shocks. The vomiting started again.[212] When the doctor examined him after this, he noted that Eugene was badly

----

209. Report of H.F.J. Schumann, Office of District Surgeon, September 19, 1985.

210. Statement of Eugene Vusi Dlamini, September 18, 1985.

211. Report of H.F.J. Schuman, September 19, 1985.

212. Statement of Eugene Vusi Dlamini, September 18, 1985.

bruised and in great pain. The boy was also sluggish and disoriented.[213]

The next day, September 3, Eugene was transferred to a hospital under police guard. He was still vomiting, in extreme pain and severely depressed. When the district surgeon next saw him 16 days later, pursuant to the court order, he found Eugene still to be sluggish and in such pain that he could hardly stand. He said he had been grabbed by the hair and his head was beaten against the wall at the police station. The examining psychiatrist described him as being in acute fear of the police and bordering on a mental breakdown. The district surgeon's report also notes, "the road to recovery from considerable physical and psychic trauma will be a long and difficult one."[214]

Eugene had to spend about four weeks in the hospital. He told the Lawyers Committee, with some relief, that he was not interrogated during this time but was constantly guarded by two policemen. His mother was allowed to see him in the hospital but was not permitted to speak to him.[215] While he was in the hospital he was formally "released" from detention under Section 29 of the ISA, but immediately was charged with public violence and was kept under police guard. He eventually was released from the hospital when a successful bail application was brought on his behalf. Eugene still faces a trial in April 1986 on the public violence charge.

C. Long-Term Psychological Damage

The experience of arrest, indefinite detention and interrogation is deeply disturbing for any detainee, but can be acutely traumatic for children. A psychiatrist involved in the treatment of detainees on their release has estimated that as many as 70% develop post-traumatic stress disorders and

----

213. Report of H.F.J. Schumann, September 19, 1985.

214. Id.

215. Interview by Helena Cook, Durban, November 5, 1985.

believes detained children are particularly susceptible to anxiety disorders, depression, adjustment and behavior disorders and psychotic episodes. Children frequently exhibit acute feelings of fear, guilt, isolation and depression upon their release.

Another psychiatrist states, "They are sure that they will be detained again and often express doubts of survival if this were to happen." He says, "the isolation that was experienced in detention comes home to roost and the released child expresses [his] hopeless desolation in words that express a longing to die."

In some cases the psychological damage is severe. Johnny Mashiane, aged 15, has spent a month in a psychiatric hospital since he was released from detention. Although his friends and family say that he was a normal child before his arrest, he is now unable to speak coherently and seems confused and vacant. No one really knows what happened to him in the police cells. A friend, Sam, was arrested with Johnny on July 24, 1985. They had taken a donation to the house of a school friend who had been shot dead by the police. The security forces arrived to break up the group who had gathered there, and arrested more than 80 people, including Johnny and Sam.

According to Sam, at the police station the police "told us to sit on our haunches with our heads fastened to our knees. If we lifted our heads, they hit us with sjamboks on the back of our heads." Sam and Johnny were in the same cell. Sam stated:

> The prison police beat us all the time with sjamboks. Whenever we were taken out to eat. This went on for 14 days.
>
> Everyday the police came to interrogate us. They hit, kicked and slapped us and sjambokked us. They took us out to offices for interrogation one or two of us at a time.[216]

----

216. Statement, Johannesburg, 1985.

Then Johnny and some 20 others were taken to another police station for a night. When Johnny came back, according to Sam, he "was shaking and couldn't control his head. He couldn't speak properly either." He was not taken to see a doctor. Even when they were to be released, the ordeal was not over:

> I could see Johnny was still not well as he wandered around muttering, but the officials still hit him with a sjambok when he couldn't sign his name. They also hit me when I complained. They even sjamboked us as we left the prison . . . .

> I took Johnny home. Johnny is very different now. He is confused and seems to have something mentally wrong.[217]

Four months after his detention Johnny was still very sick and undergoing psychiatric examinations to try to determine what was wrong. His parents said that they had great difficulty in communicating with him and they fear that he will never fully recover.[218]

D. Supposed Safeguards Against Abuse in Detention

One provision of the state's security legislation, the Internal Security Act (ISA), provides that detainees are to be visited regularly by a district surgeon while in custody. The emergency regulations contained a similar provision.

District surgeons are medical officers employed by the State, whose duties include the examination of detainees and other prisoners upon their admission, release or transfer. They also are responsible for the general treatment and health of such prisoners while in custody.

----

217. Id.

218. Interview by Helena Cook, Johannesburg, November 25, 1985.

In view of the widespread allegations of torture of political detainees, it reasonably can be assumed that many district surgeons frequently detect evidence of physical abuse of detainees by police without taking any remedial action.[219] Dr. Wendy Orr's testimony in the Port Elizabeth interdict case (see Section B, *supra*) was startling precisely because district surgeons have not been outspoken about the abuse of detainees for whom they were reponsible.

Their silence has a profound effect upon the ability of detainees to mount a successful prosecution for police misconduct. Detainees held pursuant to the ISA can be held indefinitely in solitary confinement, allowing the physical evidence of torture to heal before a detainee is released. Accordingly, it is practically impossible to bring a successful prosecution against the police upon the victim's release from detention without the medical evidence of the doctor who examined him or her shortly after the abuse was inflicted.

Police and prison officials are also implicated in this conspiracy of silence. According to Dr. Orr, a number of police forms relating to allegations of assault against patients she had examined were later found to have disappeared. One young detainee, who had been so brutally assaulted that he had to be brought to Dr. Orr in a wheel chair, subsequently disappeared. Dr. Orr had specifically requested to examine the victim again after a few days, but was later told he had been discharged from prison, apparently without the required medical examination upon release.

Considerable pressure has been exerted by members of the medical profession in South Africa to enable detainees to be examined by independent rather than state-employed doctors. It finally was announced at the end of

----

219. On occasion, district surgeons have even omitted to ensure detainees receive adequate medical care for their injuries. After the appalling death in detention of the Black Consciousness leader, Steve Biko, in 1977, there were repeated calls for an investigation of the conduct of the two doctors who had examined Biko shortly before his death. Such an investigation was resisted by the Medical Association of South Africa until compelled to do so by a Supreme Court order in 1985, eight years after Biko's death. As a result of the investigation one doctor was struck off the medical roll and his assistant was found guilty of "unprofessional conduct."

1985 that detainees would be able to select doctors from a prescribed panel if they were dissatisfied with their treatment by the district surgeon.

This move has been strongly criticized by others in the medical profession because it does not address the root of the problem: the system of indefinite *incommunicado* detention and the lack of effective supervision or curbs on the police in their treatment of detainees. Moreover, detainees still are not entitled to see a doctor of their choice, but must choose from a pre-determined panel. Also, detainees themselves must take the initiative to exercise this right. While undergoing the terrifying and dehumanizing experience of detention, interrogation and torture, a detainee may be physically or mentally incapable of doing so. Children in detention, who rarely know their rights and are hardly capable of exercising them fully, will remain at particularly serious risk. For them, this new provision is unlikely to provide much protection from abuse.

CHAPTER VIII

Deaths in Detention

Some 75 people have died in police custody or shortly after their release since detention without trial was authorized by law in the 1960s.[220] Most of these people were detained pursuant to the Internal Security Act, and in many of these cases there was evidence that the detainee suffered serious abuse at the hands of the police prior to his death.

At least 12 persons died in detention during 1985, the highest number recorded for any year. Of these, three were children. One of them, Johannes Spogter, was only 13 years old.

Johannes Spogter lived in Vuyolwethu, a small rural black township outside Steytlerville in the Eastern Cape, some distance from Port Elizabeth. Up to the time of his death in July 1985, the township had been quiet, relatively untouched by the unrest erupting in the urban townships on the outskirts of Port Elizabeth. The roots of political organization were being laid in the Vuyolwethu community, however. A number of young people in the township had, only weeks before, joined together to form the Steytlerville Youth Congress, the leaders of which included 20 year-old Mzwandile Miggels. When they learned of the deaths of four well-known community leaders in Cradock, whose mutilated, charred bodies had been found some days after their mysterious disappearance, the young people in Steytlerville organized a protest demonstration.

Police immediately dispersed the march with tear gas. No one was seriously injured. Once the marchers returned to the township, however, armed police moved in to conduct a house-to-house search. According to one resident who witnessed the search, a confrontation quickly ensued. Shots rang out and Miggels lay dead. Thirteen year-old Johannes, who was injured in the shooting, ran inside his house, trying to shelter behind his grandmother. However, police stormed into the house, loaded Johannes into a police van and drove off. No one knows what happened to Johannes while in custody, but two days later his relatives were informed that he had died in the police cells. The shocked community held a funeral for Johannes and Mzwandile Miggels on July 13. One resident told the

----

220. See Deaths in Detention and South Africa's Security Laws, Lawyers Committee for Civil Rights Under Law, September 1983.

Lawyers Committee, "Nothing like this has ever happened here before. We are all angry. This township will never be the same again."[221]

Thembalake George, aged 15, was at home in Ginsberg, King Williams Town when some students, pursued by the police, burst in seeking refuge on August 15, 1985. The students had been singing freedom songs when police arrived to break up the crowd. The police sjambokked[222] all the young people in the house and arrested them on the charge of attending an illegal gathering. Thembalake was also arrested, despite his protests and those of his family that he was not part of the group that the police had been chasing.

Refused permission to see her son at the police station the next day, his mother later found him in Gray Hospital under police guard. He was unconscious and his face was badly swollen. She heard a doctor tell the police that the boy should be transferred immediately to another hospital. By the time the ambulance arrived, however, Thembalake had died without regaining consciousness.[223]

The third child to die in detention last year was 16 year-old Meshack Mogale from Mamelodi East, outside Pretoria. Meshack was attending the customary night vigil on November 15 for another unrest victim, Magdeline Nkoane. The police arrived to break up the vigil, as they frequently do, and arrested a number of the mourners, including Meshack. His sister, Betty, was also arrested. She later stated that Meshack was kicked and sjambokked by police at the time of the arrest. Two days later, Meshack died in Kalafong hospital. Nothing further is known of the circumstances of his death, which was confirmed by police.[224]

No one has been prosecuted for any of these deaths. Nor is there any indication that investigations are being vigorously pursued.

----

221. Interviews by Helena Cook, Vuyolwethu township, July 13, 1985.

222. As noted elsewhere, a sjambok is a metal-tipped whip.

223. "Thembalake's Death," Crisis News, Western Province Council of Churches, October 1985.

224. November 1985 Report Detainees' Parents Support Committee.

CHAPTER IX

Conditions in Detention

A. General Conditions

South African prisons are a harsh environment for a child. Already severely overcrowded,[225] their capacity has been further strained by the huge influx of political prisoners during the unrest.

By law, unsentenced juveniles are not supposed be detained in prison or a police cell unless such detention is "necessary" and no other "suitable place of detention" is available.[226] In fact, however, large numbers of children have been detained in the ordinary prisons, and those detained during the unrest have been treated the same as adults.

The latest statistics indicate that there were just over 2000 unsentenced juveniles under the age of 19 years in prison at the end of January 1986.[227] This represents an enormous increase over 1984, before the current unrest really took hold. An official survey in March 1984 revealed that there were 570 unsentenced juveniles aged between 10 and 17 years old in prison at that time; 97% of them were black.[228] Emergency detainees interviewed by the Lawyers Committee reported that they had shared cells with

----

225. South Africa has one of the highest prison populations in the world and in 1983 faced prison overcrowding by 46%, according to the government-appointed Commission of Inquiry into the Structure and Functioning of the Courts, 1983.

226. Act No. 8 of 1959, Section 29. Section 28 of the Child Care Act No. 74 of 1983 provides that the Minister may establish places of detention for the reception and detention of children awaiting trial or sentencing. The Act imposes no obligation on the Minister, however, to provide such alternatives to prison for juveniles.

227. "Apartheid Barometer," Weekly Mail, April 4-10, 1986.

228. House of Assembly Debates, June 11, 1984 cols. 1549-1574.

anywhere from 16 to 40 detainees, of whom a number were children under 12 years old.[229]

Although the Prisons Act requires that unsentenced juveniles generally be separated from adults,[230] many children detained under the emergency regulations were not. Also, a number of children in custody on criminal charges have been placed in cells with ordinary criminals, with serious consequences.

Eleven year-old Fanie Goduka was held for seven weeks in a cell with 13 adult criminals when he was arrested and charged with public violence, allegedly for throwing stones at a motor vehicle.[231] He told the Lawyers Committee:

> I was taken in a hippo [armored vehicle] by some soldiers. They hit me with their fists and hit my face with sticks. At first I was alone in a cell and I had to sign a statement. They said they would beat me up if I didn't sign it. After I appeared in court they put me in a cell with 13 adult criminals. I was beaten there especially by the criminals who brought our food. They beat anyone who did not give them money.[232]

Another two boys, Martin and Steven (both 17), were arrested in Alexandra on December 19, 1985 on charges of public violence. Both boys were badly assaulted by the

----

229. Interviews by Helena Cook, Johannesburg and Cape Town, November 1985.

230. Section 23 of the Prisons Act states that unsentenced juveniles are not to be permitted to associate with adult criminals unless the other person is a co-accused or the association would not be detrimental to the child. It should be noted that s.1 of the Prisons Act defines a "juvenile" as a person under the age of 21 years so that juvenile cells may properly contain people up to this age.

231. See Chapter VI.B., supra.

232. Interview by Helena Cook, Johannesburg, November 22, 1985.

police[233] and were then held in a cell with adult criminals. Martin stated, "We were kept with eight criminals who beat me up the whole night, until we moved into another cell."[234] Steven added, "The criminals beat me up and took my shoes and trousers."[235]

One detainee held at Diepkloof Prison in Johannesburg has alleged that, during his detention, the common criminals who distributed food had persuaded young boys aged between 14 and 20 to have sex with them in exchange for more food. The same detainee was also asked by a judge who visited the prison to take a 14 year-old "under his wing" because the boy was distressed, and had asked the judge to take him home.[236]

A number of children have described a variety of severe punishments to which they were subjected if they were too noisy or made complaints or sometimes for no apparent reason at all. Prison guards beat children with sjamboks; released tear gas into closed cells; turned on high-pressure water hoses into the cells, soaking the children and their bedding; and deprived detainees of meals. A 14 year-old child detained in Bongolethu township after disturbances described his treatment there:

> We were making our beds and tidying up, but they said we were slow and they sprayed tear gas into the cell. And then later they sprayed water which made the blankets and mats wet. When they sprayed tear gas, they locked us in a closed cell. Some of us fainted and some of us vomited. I vomited. The others with me in the cell were all young; one was 9 years old, others 10 and 11 years . . . . Sometimes

----

233. See Chapter VII.A., supra.

234. Statement, Johannesburg, January 1985.

235. Statement, Johannesburg, January 1985.

236. Affidavit, Johannesburg, August 30, 1985.

the policemen came at night and kicked us
and woke us up.[237]

Many children have reported that they were not
allowed out of the cells, except at meal times. A
memorandum written and signed by 50 emergency detainees
and smuggled out of Diepkloof Prison stated, "Except for
meal times, we are locked up in the cells for 23 hours a day,
leading to the heightening of tension and frustration among
detainees." Another ex-detainee, Elias (aged 15), told the
Lawyers Committee:

> While I was in prison we were not allowed
> out of the cells at all. We had a Bible but no
> other reading material and no games. They
> told us we were "small ANC"[238] and could not
> be let out of the cells.[239]

A number of children said that they were not given
food, or even water in some cases, during the first day or so
of their arrest while they were being moved from one police
station to another or to a prison. An 11 year-old boy,
arrested in Dobsonville on November 1, 1985, told the
Lawyers Committee:

> In the morning [Saturday] the police came to
> count us. Food was brought to us. It was
> stale bread and tea and was so bad we
> couldn't eat it. We asked for water and they
> refused to give us any.[240]

Later that day he was moved to another police station:

> On Saturday night at Meadowlands we were
> given the first water. No food. We slept. In

----

237. Statement, Bongolethu, December 28, 1985.

238. This refers to the banned political organization, the African National
Congress.

239. Interview by Helena Cook, Johannesburg, November 25, 1985.

240. Interview by Helena Cook, Johannesburg, November 25, 1985.

the morning we were given soft porridge and
black tea. At lunch we were given pap and
black tea. For supper, peas with the pods
still on and pap. I became sick with a bad
tummy.[241]

Another young detainee, Gavin (17 years), told the Lawyers
Committee that he and the others in his cell were forced to
drink from the toilet bowl because the police refused to give
them water.[242]

The Diepkloff detainees' memorandum complained
of the monotonous, poor diet and the practice of giving
different diets to the various racial groups. "African
detainees, for instance, do not receive the same quantity of
bread," they noted and, "white detainees receive a far
superior diet than Black detainees." For meals, "detainees
are forced to squat on the cold cement floor." Detainees at
one police station allegedly received nothing but soft
porridge three times a day. Many suffered a drastic weight
loss.

B. Access to Detainees

Access to young detainees by their families or
lawyers has been of crucial importance in ascertaining their
safety and well-being. Nevertheless, children (like others)
held pursuant to the Internal Security Act (ISA) are
generally held incommunicado in solitary confinement.
Detainees held for interrogation under Section 29 of the ISA
are, by law, supposed to receive regular visits from
magistrates and inspectors. These provisions were
incorporated into the security legislation in 1982 to respond
to widespread allegations of assault and torture of ISA
detainees. There were no such provisions in the special
rules drawn up for emergency detainees. Yet large numbers
of such detainees also complained of abuse during detention.

----

241. Statement, Johannesburg, November 11, 1985.

242. Interview by Helena Cook, Cape Town, November 19, 1985.

Special rules laid down for emergency detainees provided that no detainee could be visited by anyone without permission of the prison commander, acting with the concurrence of the Police Commissioner. In practice, it was the local police who took charge of visiting rights. A permit to visit had to be obtained from the local police where the arrest took place, and only applications from immediate family members were considered. In many cases visits were denied. Permission, once granted, was valid for one visit only. Lawyers were required to obtain special permission from the Minister of Law and Order or the Police Commissioner in order to see detainees. These requests were denied in practically all cases.

The visiting policy for emergency detainees differed both from prison to prison and according to race. The Detainees' Parents Support Committee (DPSC) has noted that white emergency detainees were allowed to have regular visits, while most black detainees were refused visits and some were even refused fresh clothing for weeks. The mother of one 11 year-old African boy, Sonny, broke down and wept as she recounted to the Lawyers Committee her long and expensive journey out to Victor Verster prison outside Cape Town in a state of great anxiety about her young son. When she finally arrived at the prison, she was refused entry because she had not known that she needed a police permit.[243]

A prison officer had to be in sight and hearing of the detainee and the visitor, and no physical contact was allowed. Visitors were separated by an iron grille or glass panel, which is particularly distressing for younger children. A priest detained in Victor Verster prison in Cape Town told the Lawyers Committee:

> One little boy was visited by his mother and neither of them could say a word. Throughout the entire visit, he sat on one side of the panel, crying, while she sat and wept on the other side.[244]

----

243. Interview by Helena Cook, Cape Town, November 19, 1985.

244. Interview by Helena Cook, Cape Town, November 17, 1985.

Emergency detainees were supposed to be examined by a district surgeon on admission and "regularly" thereafter.[245]   Treatment by an independent doctor, a specialist or in a hospital was permitted only on the recommendation of the district surgeon, acting with the concurrence of the Police Commissioner.   Detainees complained that medical treatment was often perfunctory or non-existent, even after serious assault.

In the face of increasing allegations of assault and torture, a number of judges of the Supreme Court began to visit detainees, as did a group of opposition members of Parliament from the Progressive Federalist Party.   Even this proved to be a highly inadequate safeguard.   Black detainees were reluctant to make complaints either because they did not perceive these white figures of authority as being truly independent, or because they feared reprisals from the police for having voiced complaints.   Most of the reports of torture and assault came to light only after fellow detainees were released, or notes from prison were smuggled out.

----

245. Rules for Emergency Detainees No. 20(1).

CHAPTER X

Investigation and Prosecution of Abuses
by the Security Forces

There is little possibility of adequate recourse against the security forces when a child is injured or killed, or in the event of wrongful arrest and assault while in custody. The security forces are demonstrably unwilling to pursue vigorous investigations and prosecutions of their own members. There is no independent body to whom complaints can be made and the government has ignored calls to set up a commission of inquiry into police and army conduct during the unrest. Since much of the abuse takes place in police and prison cells it is very difficult to gather evidence to support a victim's allegations. Civil proceedings against the security forces are lengthy and many victims cannot afford the legal costs involved.

The South African government strongly defends its security forces and protests that they act "within civilized norms." Indeed, the government makes every effort to protect the police and army from legal investigations and public scrutiny. During the State of Emergency, as well as imposing a ban on press reporting of their conduct, the State President granted the security forces a blanket indemnity preventing civil or criminal prosecutions against them for all acts taken "in good faith." The emergency regulations established a presumption of good faith until the contrary was proven. This placed a heavy onus of proof on the complainant that, in the prevailing situation of conflict and disorder, was almost impossible to discharge. The indemnity was extended in October 1985 to cover the whole country, not merely areas affected by the Emergency.

This indemnity, while far-reaching, is not without precedent. Section 103 ter. of the Defense Act[246] provides that members of the SADF or any other person acting in the service of the state enjoy an indemnity from civil or

----

246. Act No. 44 of 1957.

criminal proceedings for acts "advised, commanded or done in good faith" in connection with the prevention or suppression of terrorism in an operational area. The Minister of Defense can effectively halt any legal proceedings if he is of the opinion that the acts in question were done in good faith. A certificate signed by the Minister to the effect that the acts were carried out under command constitutes conclusive proof that they fall within the indemnity.

Recently, some attempted legal challenges to detentions have frequently been pre-empted by the police, who simply release the detainee before the matter reaches the court. This avoids the possibility of a Supreme Court precedent that could be the basis for relief for other detainees.

A. Complaints

The standard response of the police to allegations of their misconduct has been to require complainants to lodge a sworn affidavit with the police. This means that complaints will be investigated in effect by those responsible for the alleged misconduct.

The security forces are deeply mistrusted by township residents, who perceive them not as the protectors of law and order, but as representatives of a white minority regime bent on repression. In the absence of any independent body to undertake investigations of police brutality, victims are reluctant to come forward, fearing reprisals will be taken against them or their families and having little confidence in the willingness of the police to enforce internal discipline within their ranks.

Indeed, there has been little evidence of any attempts so far to pursue a rigorous investigation when complaints are made and the police are generally unsympathetic and even abusive to complainants. Even the Police Commissioner, General Coetzee, has referred to them as "so-called witnesses who calculatedly spread false and twisted reports bent on making the SAP villains."[247]

In response to increasing complaints against members of the SADF in the townships, more than two dozen offices were opened in September 1985 to receive and investigate complaints specifically against the SADF. Here, too, residents said they feared reprisals by the soldiers, and by November only sixteen complaints had been made. One case under investigation concerned a 12 year-old Soweto boy suffering from cancer who was picked up by soldiers.[248]

In February this year it was disclosed in Parliament by the Ministers of Law and Order and Defense that, out of more than 500 complaints lodged against the security forces concerning actions in unrest areas, only one policeman had subsequently been convicted. Disciplinary steps had been taken against seven policemen and eight national servicemen.[249]

B. The Government's Response

In general, the government has not intervened or even evidenced concern about such complaints and has consistently ignored pleas to hold a top-level inquiry into police and army conduct during the unrest. An exception, and not a very encouraging one, occurred last year after police opened fire on a funeral crowd in Langa on March 21, 1985, killing at least 20 mourners and injuring many others. Most of the victims were shot in the back. Following an international outcry, a commission of inquiry into the incident was hastily set up under a Supreme Court judge, Mr. Justice Kannemeyer. While very critical of police conduct, the commission did not find that any individuals could be held responsible and no disciplinary actions were taken.

----

247. "SA Police Chief: give us facts," Daily Dispatch, July 9, 1985.

248. "SADF received only 16 complaints," Sowetan, November 26, 1985.

249. "Police, SADF: 500 Complaints," Cape Times, February 17, 1986.

A similar incident occurred in Mamelodi eight months later, leaving 19 people dead but attracting far less public attention than Langa, largely as a result of severe restrictions enforced by the police with regard to the press reporting of the incident. On this occasion, calls for a commission of inquiry were rejected out of hand by the government.[250]

In September 1985, a U.S. official said that the Reagan Administration would press South Africa to create a "more independent body for examining complaints." It was hoped that this would enable blacks to register complaints about police brutality without fear of harassment. However, no apparent progress on this initiative has been made so far.

In March 1986, the Committee of Concern for Children presented the Minister of Law and Order with a memorandum detailing the ill-treatment of children in detention prepared from statements made by former detainees. The memorandum, endorsed by more than fifteen human rights, child welfare, medical and civic groups, stated, "An analysis of the statements does not indicate isolated incidents where one policeman oversteps the mark, but rather a consistent pattern that is occurring countrywide."

The Minister dismissed the memorandum as being unsubstantiated, untested and one-sided. He criticized the fact that the names and addresses of the victims were omitted, although this was a necessary precautionary measure to protect the victims from further harassment and abuse by police. Mrs. Helen Suzman, a member of the parliamentary opposition group, the Progressive Federalist Party, has said that the facts could be established if a judicial commission of inquiry were set up to investigate police torture of detainees.

----

250. An independent commission of inquiry has been set up by the Pretoria Council of Churches but this Commission has no authority to subpoena police witnesses.

C. Legal Proceedings

Criminal prosecutions of the conduct of the security forces are extremely rare, even in the face of substantial evidence of abuse. The case of four year-old Mitah Ngobeni, killed by a rubber bullet, was described earlier in Chapter III.A. At the inquest the magistrate found that no one could be held directly responsible for her death even though the evidence of the policeman who fired the fatal shot was contradicted by a witness. Prosecutions of police following deaths of detainees while in detention or shortly after their release are practically unknown.[251]

Even when cases of abuse by the security forces are successfully prosecuted, sentences are often unduly lenient. In December 1985, two Uitenhage detectives were convicted of assault of an 18 year-old youth after members of the human rights organization, Black Sash, had walked in as detectives were beating the youth while he was lying down shackled to a table leg. The detectives were fined only R150 (about $75) and were suspended pending an inquiry into their fitness to serve in the force.[252] One month earlier, eight members of the SADF were convicted of the intentional and unprovoked assault of a black man in New Brighton. They had branded his legs with heated iron bars, pelted him with stones, kicked him repeatedly in the stomach and beaten him with a piece of wood. They were each sentenced to a fine of R200 (about $100) or four months' imprisonment.[253]

Civil proceedings for damages can sometimes be brought against the police with a greater degree of success but this procedure can be very lengthy and many black applicants are unable to afford a lawyer to bring a civil

----

251. The conviction of a policeman for culpable homicide in 1984, after a detainee was shot at pointblank range, has been the only successful prosecution out of more than 75 deaths in detention during the past 20 years.

252. Reply of the Minister of Law and Order Louis Le Grange to a Parliamentary Question, February 1986.

253. "Eight SADF men who assaulted African Sentenced," Eastern Province Herald, November 5, 1985.

action. When such cases are brought, a great many of them are settled out of court. There was a significant increase in the amount paid out in such claims by the police in financial year 1984/85. About R1,4 million was paid out as compared with R692,000 in the previous financial year 1983/84.[254]

One of the major difficulties in pursuing legal proceedings against the security forces lies in the gathering of evidence. Much of the abuse takes place in police or prison cells or inside armored vehicles, out of sight of potential witnesses. As noted in Chapter VII.D. *supra*, district surgeons who are responsible for the medical care of detainees have not generally shown themselves willing to give evidence of police abuse and torture.

A recent decision of the Supreme Court in the Eastern Cape in January 1986, has provided lawyers with a potentially new legal weapon with which to pursue allegations of torture by police that may prove to be of assistance in gathering the necessary evidence. The applicants in the case were six ex-detainees who had suffered torture by electric shock and beating while being held in police stations in East London. An application to the court was made *in camera*, without prior notification to the police, seeking to permit the applicants to conduct an immediate search of the police stations for the instruments of torture.

The court upheld in principle the right of torture victims to carry out such a search without alerting the police. This exceptional type of order, that has been generally limited in South Africa to commercial cases, is available where the court accepts that there is probability that vital evidence will be destroyed if the defendants are given prior warning of the search. The application in this particular case was refused on the grounds that the applicants already had sufficient evidence of torture and that the requested search was not necessary in order for justice to be done. Nevertheless, the establishment of the

----

254. "Police pay out R1,4m in claims for damages," Sunday Tribune, December 9, 1985.

principle may prove to be of significant assistance in future cases where torture is alleged.

CHAPTER XI

Operation of the Justice System

South Africa's Constitution relegates the nation's courts to a subservient role within the government, leaving them virtually powerless to strike down duly enacted laws, however repressive. The security laws further constrict the courts' ability to protect fundamental human rights, and the emergency regulations exacerbated this problem. Political considerations play a significant role in the appointment of judges, and many have been unwilling to undermine the power of the Executive in security-related cases, even within the narrow straits they navigate.[255]

In a few recent cases, however, some judges have asserted a more significant role in protecting individual liberties and curtailing the enormous discretion of the state in security-related matters. These judicial inroads into the vast power wielded by the Executive -- in areas where many believed the state could not be challenged -- are virtually unprecedented.

A. Structure of the South African Judiciary

The Supreme Court of South Africa consists of an Appellate Division, the highest tribunal, and ten provincial and local divisions that sit both as courts of first instance and as courts of appeal from the lower magistrates' courts.[256] Supreme Court judges are appointed by the State

----

255. Professor John Dugard of the University of Witwatersrand, a leading expert in the field of human rights, has estimated that more than half of South Africa's judges could be described as supporters of the ruling Nationalist Party. See Human Rights and the South African Legal Order, John Dugard, 1977. Also, in his studies of political trials between 1978 and 1982, he found that the same few judges were hearing practically all the political cases. According to his research, 17% of the judiciary heard 84% of these cases and four judges heard over 50% of them.

256. Magistrates' courts have a limited civil and criminal jurisdiction and are restricted in the sentences that can be imposed.

President-in-Council (the Cabinet) from the ranks of senior practising lawyers. They have security of tenure up to age 70 and can be removed only for misbehavior or incapacity. All of the Supreme Court judges are white.

The South African Constitution provides that Parliament is supreme and that the courts have virtually no power to overturn legislation duly enacted by Parliament. South Africa has no Bill of Rights, leaving the courts little opportunity to uphold individual rights and liberties against the power of the state.

B. Detention and Banning Cases

In recent months, South African courts have afforded some measure of relief to petitioners in cases involving detention and banning. At the end of 1984, for example, the Natal Provincial Division of the Supreme Court ordered the release of seven security detainees, having found that warrants issued for their preventive detention pursuant to Section 28 of the ISA[257] were fatally defective because reasons for the detention were not given and no explanation as to why the reasons could not be disclosed was provided. This decision was recently upheld by the Appellate Division. On the same day as the appeal was upheld, the Rand Supreme Court ordered the release of four others detained under Section 28.

In 1985, again in Natal, detainees held for interrogation pursuant to Section 29 of the ISA were ordered released by the Supreme Court. This section had always been regarded as one of the most impregnable of the security provisions. It authorizes detentions where the detaining officer has "reason to believe" that the detainee has committed or intends to commit an offense or is withholding information about an offense. The court held in two Section 29 cases that the detentions were invalid because the detaining officers had not proved that they had a factual basis for their belief that the detentions were warranted. The state attempted to rely on the clause in Section 29 that

----

257. See Chapter II.D., supra.

ousts judicial review. Nevertheless, the court held that, without adequate proof of the factual basis for the belief that the detention was warranted, the detention did not properly fall within the terms of the section, rendering the ouster clause inoperative.

These decisions had a significant impact. A number of other Section 29 detainees were released by the state before a similar court application for their release could be brought.

Another application was brought in Natal in September 1985 for the release of a Section 29 detainee on psychological grounds. The detainee had been admitted to a hospital for psychiatric treatment following his interrogation while in incommunicado detention. His attorneys argued that, since the petitioner was no longer fit to answer questions, his detention "for the purposes of interrogation" was invalid. The state initially opposed the application calling an expert witness who claimed that the detainee should be sent back to the cells for continued interrogation. However, while the court action was still pending, the Minister of Law and Order suddenly released the detainee, acknowledging that further detention might severely impair his mental health. The issue that the court was asked to address affects many Section 29 detainees. Although the section states that these detainees are to be released when they have answered all questions "satisfactorily" (unless they are to be charged), many detainees held pursuant to this provision report that they are held beyond the period of interrogation.

Section 30 of the ISA grants the Attorney General the power to override the court's traditional jurisdiction to grant bail in security cases involving treason by issuing a certificate refusing bail. Such a certificate was issued in March 1985 in a major treason trial of 16 United Democratic Front leaders in Pietermaritzburg, Natal. In a strong decision, the Supreme Court held that the certificate was improperly drafted and invalid. The judge also attacked the practice of issuing such certificates as being a "serious inroad into the traditional role of the courts," and as placing the Attorney General, an executive appointee, in the position of being a judge in his own cause. Although the Attorney General could have issued a revised certificate, he did not do so and all the defendants were released on bail.[258]

Later in the year, an Attorney General's certificate was also thrown out by the Pretoria Supreme Court in another large treason trial of 22 defendants, currently underway in Delmas. In this case, however, bail was denied on the merits of a later application.

The most recent successful challenge to the stringent provisions of the ISA was filed in March 1986. The case involved the state's practice of imposing banning orders on individuals. A banning order was imposed on a United Democratic Front leader in Port Elizabeth in March. The order was overturned by the Supreme Court on the grounds that the State had given insufficient reasons for issuing the order. This judgement opened the way for challenges of other outstanding banning orders drafted in similar terms.[259] Two other successful court applications were brought for the lifting of banning orders and were unopposed by the state. A further two individuals had their banning orders lifted before the matter reached the courts. One of these individuals was the longest serving banned person in the country and had been banned for 26 years.

The effect of these historic Supreme Court decisions, many of them based largely on technical arguments, could easily be undermined in the future by greater care on the part of the Executive to ensure that warrants and other notices or certificates provided for in the ISA are issued in strict conformity with the requirements laid down in the Act. That is precisely what happened following a recent case in the Transvaal. The Supreme Court there held that a notice, issued annually since 1976 by the Minister of Law and Order banning all outdoor meetings pursuant to Section 46 of the ISA, was invalid. The Minister immediately issued

----

258. The charges against 12 of the defendants in this case were dropped by the State in December 1985 after the disastrous performance of the main prosecution witness.

259. Under the South African judicial system, a Supreme Court judgement acts as a binding precedent in later cases within the same provincial division (unless overturned on appeal) and is of persuasive value in other provincial divisions.

a new banning notice with the requisite change of wording in accordance with the court's decision. Nevertheless, it is significant that the seemingly impregnable provisions of the ISA have been successfully attacked in the courts, and these cases represent a welcome move by some judges toward requiring a greater measure of accountability by the Executive in security matters.

A number of challenges to the emergency regulations were also brought before the courts during the State of Emergency. In one notable case in the Eastern Cape the court upheld the basic right of a detainee, whose detention was extended beyond the initial 14-day period, to be heard in his own defense and to make representations as to why his further detention may have been unnecessary. The judgement cast doubt on the validity of the detentions of all emergency detainees then being held for longer than 14 days.

However, the State's response to this judgement was indicative of its ability and readiness to bypass the judicial system. The State President immediately issued revised regulations that expressly denied detainees the right to make representations or even to receive notice when their detention was extended.[260] Nevertheless, the case indicated that some judges were willing to examine the regulations despite the attempts by the Executive to oust all judicial intervention in respect of the emergency measures by means of a broad indemnity provision in the regulations.[261]

C. Cases Involving Physical Abuse of Detainees

Of potentially greater significance are a number of urgent interdicts granted by the courts last year enjoining the police from further assaulting detainees. The interdict is a form of injunctive relief afforded when it is considered likely that further assaults may take place.

----

260. Proclamation R207, Government Gazette No. 10003, October 31, 1985.

261. See Chapter II.F., supra.

The most well known case in which an urgent interdict has been granted was heard in Port Elizabeth in September 1985 in response to an application filed by a district surgeon, Dr. Wendy Orr, and 43 others. The far-reaching order issued by the judge in that case enjoined the police from assaulting all present and future detainees in two Port Elizabeth prisons.[262] Most cases in which urgent interdicts have been granted are still pending, awaiting a full hearing on the merits. It remains to be seen whether they will lead to prosecutions of individual police officers for torture and assault.

Another decision of the Supreme Court in East London has also focused attention on the practice of torture by the South African police. In a case brought by six former detainees who had been subjected to various forms of torture during their detention, the court upheld in principle the right of torture victims in certain circumstances to search police premises for implements of torture without prior notification to the State.[263] It is to be hoped that this may facilitate the bringing of civil claims against the police by torture victims, and thereby act as a curb on the police in the future.

----

262. See Chapter VII.B., supra.

263. See Chapter X.B., supra.

CHAPTER XII

The Role of the United States

In a major foreign policy speech delivered on March 15, 1986, President Reagan stated, "We have sought to defend and advance the cause of democracy, freedom and human rights throughout the world." U.S. policy toward South Africa demonstrates no such defense of human rights, freedom or democracy for the country's beleaguered black majority. When Assistant Secretary of State for African Affairs, Chester Crocker, testified at a recent congressional hearing on South Africa, he expressed the Administration's support for "majority rule." This position was hastily retracted by Administration officials who said that Crocker had gone too far and that his statement had not been approved by the White House.

The Reagan Administration's policy toward South Africa has met with bitter criticism both in South Africa and in the United States. The South African National Education Crisis Committee, set up in late 1985 by parents, teachers and students in an attempt to address the educational crisis resulting from the unrest and boycotts, stated in March 1986, "We consider the Reagan Administration as an accomplice in the crimes of apartheid."

In the face of the increasing anger and frustration of the black majority toward the intractable Botha regime and the escalating violence and repression in the country, the Reagan Administration has continued throughout the civil unrest to hold fast to the basic principles and tactics of its policy of "constructive engagement." The policy relies on quiet diplomacy and moral persuasion, rather than forceful criticism, to promote "peaceful change" in South Africa and an end to apartheid.

Constructive engagement was conceived essentially as a regional policy to promote stability and security and minimize Soviet influence in southern Africa. In order to secure the South African government's essential cooperation in the achievement of these regional objectives, the U.S. has been careful to minimize confrontation with the regime over its internal policies and consequently has not spoken out forcefully on human rights issues.

A. Support for a "Reformist" Government

The Administration has been quick to voice approval and support for the "reformist" policies of President Botha's government, despite the fact that the more significant reforms that have been proposed are little more than undefined promises, and those that have been instituted do not begin to address the fundamental grievances of the black majority. In March last year, the Administration stated that "a genuine process of reform is underway in South Africa" and described the government as "determined to move down the road of constructive change away from apartheid." Later in the year President Reagan praised these "reformist" policies and asserted, incorrectly, that "they have eliminated the segregation we once had in our own country."

In August 1985, a high-level meeting between top U.S. officials and the South African Foreign Minister fueled expectations that major new reforms were imminent. These hopes were dashed when President Botha gave a long-awaited speech that made only vague promises of "reform" and took a strongly aggressive line against his opponents. The U.S. described the speech, which was strongly criticized throughout the international community, as "an important statement" that discussed "some issues at the core of the problem of apartheid." When Nobel Peace laureate, Bishop Desmond Tutu, in protest against the speech, refused to join a delegation that met with President Botha, the U.S. publicly criticized the tireless anti-apartheid campaigner.

In sharp contrast to the Administration's public support for the so-called reforms promised by the South African government, it has been extremely slow and cautious to voice any criticism of the regime's increasingly brutal response to internal opposition. While condemning the violence in the townships, the Administration has been careful to lay the responsibility on all participants in the conflict. After police opened fire on a funeral procession in Langa on March 21, 1985 leaving 20 dead and many more injured, most of them shot in the back, President Reagan said:

> There is an element in South Africa that do
> not want a peaceful settlement of this, who
> want a violent settlement, who want trouble
> in the streets and this is what's going on.

When the State of Emergency was declared, it was six days before the White House reacted with a statement that merely called on South Africa to act with the "greatest restraint" and to expedite an end to the emergency.

This conciliatory and supportive policy toward a government engaging in a campaign of increasing repression and violence against its opponents, coupled with the Administration's continuing refusal to take stronger measures against the Botha regime, has led to bitter denunciations of the U.S. by large sections of the black majority in South Africa and by a growing anti-apartheid movement in the United States. Bishop Tutu said, "We will not forget where the American Administration stood at a time when we needed them desperately."

B. Limited Sanctions Are Imposed

Proponents of constructive engagement in the Administration held out against calls for the imposition of economic sanctions against South Africa as being anathema to the tactic of quiet persuasion and likely to impose economic hardship on the black majority they were trying to help.   However, faced with a U.S. congressional bill mandating sanctions and the likelihood that a presidential veto of the legislation would be overridden, President Reagan finally signed an Executive Order imposing limited economic sanctions in September 1985.   At the same time, the Administration was quick to point out that this did not imply a reversal of the former policy, now termed "active constructive engagement."

The sanctions imposed include a prohibition on computer and nuclear exports to South Africa, a ban on loans to the South African government and on the sale of Krugerrands and measures to persuade U.S. companies in

South Africa to comply with a code of conduct based on the Sullivan principles. The impact of the sanctions was considerably diminished by the simultaneous resumption of full diplomatic relations with Pretoria and the return of the U.S. ambassador, who had been withdrawn earlier in the year in protest against cross-border military aggression by South Africa.

C. Active Constructive Engagement

The imposition of sanctions has not generally been accompanied by any more forceful criticism by the U.S. Administration of South Africa's policies of repression and violence or the brutality of the security forces in the townships. At the end of August, the State Department did strongly denounce brutal police action against a protest march in Cape Town and the banning of COSAS. It also described the banning of individuals as an "odious" practice that "offends the democratic values of free speech and assembly." The response of the White House, however, was more muted, and stressed only the "urgent need on the part of all parties in South Africa to cease violent activity."

In general, however, there has been no public condemnation by the Administration of the official violence and widespread human rights violations in South Africa. Reports of the large-scale detentions of children, the assaults and torture of these young detainees, the indiscriminate shooting and violence with reckless disregard for life have elicited little or no comment. On the contrary, the Administration continues to reinforce its policy of quiet persuasion, and advocates continuing active engagement with the South Africans.

In testimony given recently before the House sub-committees on Africa and International Economic Policy and Trade, Assistant Secretary of State for African Affairs, Chester Crocker, stated firmly, "Our access to various groups and individuals gives us openings for using diplomacy and political and moral persuasion -- the most effective tools for us in these dangerous times." The Administration's goal was, he said, to help "an unhappy but essentially friendly nation" and to "encourage the [South African] government and other communities to open doors and to walk through them." He acknowledged that the purpose of imposing sanctions had been simply to demonstrate a rejection of apartheid and to build bipartisan support in Congress for U.S. policy toward South Africa.

The Administration continues to promote dialogue and diplomacy in the face of threats by the South African government to use greater force in the townships and tighten the already repressive web of its security legislation as well as provocative moves that fly in the face of negotiations, such as the banning of two important black community leaders in Port Elizabeth in late March 1986.

Constructive engagement has already proved to have little positive impact in persuading the Botha government to engage in meaningful negotiations with black leaders. More seriously, in the eyes of large sectors of the black majority, it has severely discredited the efforts of the United States toward bringing about an end to apartheid. The continued emphasis on the policy now threatens to undermine any further U.S. attempts to bring both sides to a position of negotiation. Bishop Tutu has repeatedly criticized the policy of the U.S. and other Western nations and has called it racist. "We're talking about children being killed by a racist Government that is protected from the consequences of its actions by Mr. Reagan, Mrs. Thatcher and Mr. Kohl," he said in October 1985. "Certainly the support of this racist policy is racist." Earlier in the year, Bishop Tutu Described constructive engagement as being "as evil, as immoral, as un-Christian as the policy they are seeking to buttress - apartheid."

MARION CAPRIOTTI
Secretary

ADDIE MOORE
Records Manager

LEMUAL THOMAS
Clerk

ELIZABETH SILVA
Receptionist

RECENT LAWYERS COMMITTEE PUBLICATIONS

Human Rights:

"*. . .In the face of cruelty" The Reagan Administration's Human Rights Record in 1984* (with Americas Watch and Helsinki Watch). January 1985, 128 pages, $8.00.

Report on Human Rights in Chile. Quarterly (with Americas Watch), $2.00.

Haiti: Rights Denied (with Americas Watch & National Coalition for Haitian Refugees). March 1985, 25 pages, $3.00.

Honduras: Crisis on the Border. November 1984, 96 pages, $6.00.

El Salvador: Justice Denied. A report on 12 human rights cases. March 1985, 55 pages, $6.00.

Free Fire: The Fifth Supplement to the Report on Human Rights in El Salvador. August 1984, 137 pages, $6.00.

Kampuchea: After the Worst. A Report on Current Violations of Human Rights. August 1985, 250 pages, $10.00.

Nicaragua: Revolutionary Justice. April 1985, 160 pages, $10.00.

Zia's Law: Human Rights Under Military Rule in Pakistan. July 1985, 116 pages, $7.00.

"Salvaging" Democracy: Human Rights in the Philippines. December 1985, 217 pages, $10.00.

Poland: Three Years After. December 1984, 105 pages, $6.00.

The War Against Children: South Africa's Youngest Victims April 1986, 151 pages, $10.00.

Mamelodi: South Africa's Response to Peaceful Protest January 1986, 33 pages, $3.00.

The Generals Give Back Uruguay. A report on human rights. February 1985, 57 pages, $5.00.

Uruguay: The End of a Nightmare? May 1984, 85 pages, $6.00.

Zimbabwe: Wages of War May 1986, 151 Pages.

Refugees and Asylum:

El Salvador's Other Victims: The War on the Displaced (with America's Watch). April 1984, 257 pages, $10.00.

Selected Problems in the Asylum Regulations Now Being Considered for Issuance for Public Comment by the INS. July 1985, 19 pages, $4.00.

Proposals Under the Immigration and Control Act of 1983. June 1983, 11 pages, $1.00.

The Refugee Eligibility Standard. June 1983, 12 pages, $1.00.

U.S. Extradition and Asylum Practice. May 1983, 20 pages, $2.00.

Training and Practice Materials:

Manual on Representing Asylum Applicants: A manual for volunteer lawyers representing asylum seekers in the United States containing all phases of the asylum adjudication process. December 1984, $15.00.

Representation of Haitian Asylum Applicants: A manual for volunteer lawyers representing Haitian asylum seekers in the United States. October 1984, $10.00.}